BUSINESS AND PUBLIC POLICY

The chapel at Young Harris College

John H. Van Vliet III

July 2012

This book was written to help people understand important concepts. While I reserve the copyright on the publication as a whole, excerpts may be freely used and copied for non-commercial purposes.

ISBN-13:   978-1478295211

ISBN-10:   147829521X

Published by CreateSpace 24 July 2012

Acknowledgment

I wish to acknowledge the remarkable support my wife, Jo Ray Van Vliet, has given me on this project and on so much more. I also acknowledge her direct contribution to the development of key ideas in this book. Her wisdom and good sense were my constant guides.

14 July 2012

John H. Van Vliet III, Ph.D.
1577 Victoria Woods Drive
Hiawassee, Georgia 30546

Table of Contents

Introduction

The late Mrs. Josephine Ray knew covered wagons as a girl. She lived to see a man walk on the moon. Her experience illustrates the astonishing rate of technological change and the stunning growth of complexity in our lives. How is one to cope with such changes?

We cannot hope to fully understand the many highly complex and changeable elements of our lives today. Instead, one should develop an understanding of broad principles and concepts so one can view present and future complexity through lenses that offer sound frames of reference to shape and support critical thinking and reasoning.

The purpose of this book is to support the effort to deal with modern and future complexity by offering a set of fundamental concepts and ideas from several fields of study. While each of these fields of study can be pursued in greater depth, it is valuable to see them in their basic forms as interdependent elements of a complex whole.

Modern life is shaped by highly complex and intertwined factors. This book presents and explores factors taken from: Economics, Political Philosophy, Business Management, American Government, Elements of Society, and Public Policy. An understanding of the fundamentals of these topics will illuminate the major influences associated with modern structures of relatively large numbers of people.

Chapter One – Introductory Economics

General

Economics is the study of the efficient allocation of scarce resources.

"Value" is a critical concept in Economics. While it is tempting to think that "value" is well-understood by anyone, the reality is that "value" differs from person to person. My daughter was delighted to exchange money for a ticket to a rock concert. She assigned higher value to the ticket than she did to the money she would pay for the ticket. I assigned much different weights or values to the ticket and to the cost of the ticket.

Creating Value: One way to understand the creation of value is to think about what happens in a free exchange. The person selling the concert ticket to my daughter thought the money was more valuable than the ticket. My daughter thought the ticket was more valuable than the money. After the free exchange, both people were better off in their own minds. There was more net "value" in the world after the exchange than there was before the exchange.

Labor Theory of Value: A competing concept is the "labor theory of value" which holds that the value of a product or service is equal to the amount of human labor required to provide the product or service. Of course, given the variable skills and energy people bring to their work, this theory runs into the major problem of trying to define some sort of a standard unit of labor. It also suffers from the problem of how to account for machines (capital) and raw materials. Marxists and certain other varieties of socialists and progressives are attracted to the labor theory of value. You can see shadows of it in the effort to establish "comparable worth" pay polices and laws.

"Money" is a medium of exchange. It serves as a store of value. When money was in the form of precious metals, such as gold or silver, one could say the value was intrinsic. Later, however, money became bits of paper that represented gold or silver. Still later, money became nothing but bits of paper or numbers in accounts. Money no longer has intrinsic value. Its utility lies in the fact that people are willing to use the bits of paper and the account numbers as a medium of exchange.

"Market" vs. "Command" vs. "Mixed": An economy based on "market' forces, or "free-market" forces, is one that allows values to be set by the interaction of many individuals acting out of their own view of relative values. A "command" or "planned" economy relies on a central authority to lay out what is to be produced and how it is to be distributed. A "mixed" economy operates as a command economy in some areas and as a market economy in others. (Caution - As it is virtually impossible to imagine a pure market economy or a pure command economy, it is tempting to offer the facile argument that all economies must be mixed economies. Such an argument would preclude our benefitting from considerations of the differences among an economy founded on market principles, an economy founded on principles of central planning, and an economy that is deliberately structured to incorporate elements of market and command economies.)

Supply and Demand: Supply is the amount of a good or service that is available for exchange at a given price. Demand is the amount of a good or a service that is sought in an exchange. These amounts vary with price and vary over time. (If you will remember your basic Algebra, you will recall the concept of a function. A function is a relationship of two factors. For instance, one can build a function to measure the pressure of water compared with the depth below the water's surface. Supply and Demand are functions as well. The Supply function compares how much of an item would be produced and brought to market at a given price point. Demand is a similar function comparing how much people would be willing to buy at a given price point.)

Key Terminology Point: "Supply" means the function showing the relationship between quantity offered and price. "Quantity supplied" means the amount that was actually sold. A similar distinction exists between "demand" and "quantity demanded."

"Supply and Demand" Curves: The "Supply and Demand" curves show the relationship of quantities demanded and quantities supplied at various prices. As you would expect, at low prices, less is offered in the market. On the other hand, at low prices, people are willing to buy (demand) more of the product or service. The opposite is true at high prices.

The market is "cleared" at the "equilibrium price" where the amount offered matches the amount demanded. The equilibrium price (or "market price") changes with changes in demand or supply.

The "Supply and Demand Curves" are ways to represent the supply function, the demand function and the relationship between the two.

The following section illustrates the supply and demand curves step-by-step.

Start by building a simple graph with a price axis and a quantity axis.

QUANTITY

Now imagine a product. If the price is high, few people will be willing to buy (demand) the product. If the price is low, many more people will be willing to buy the product. Accordingly, a line or curve representing the demand function will start at a point such as A on the sketch and move down and to the right to reach point B on the sketch.

Each point of the Demand curve shows the quantity that would be demanded (the quantity people would be willing to buy) at that price point.

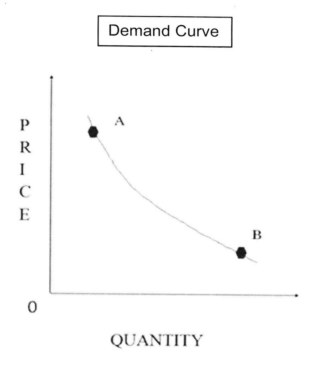

Demand Curve

QUANTITY

People who are willing to make and sell the product are enthusiastic about doing so if the price is high, and not eager to do so at low prices. Accordingly, a line or curve representing the supply function will start at a point such as C on the sketch and move up and to the right to point D. Each point on the Supply curve shows the quantity that would be made available at the given price point.

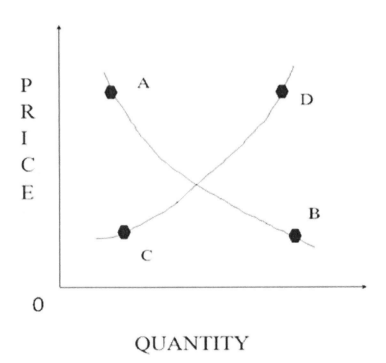

Notice what happens at the point where the two curves
intersect, Point E. That point identifies a price where the
quantity demanded is equal to the quantity supplied. The
market for that product is in equilibrium.

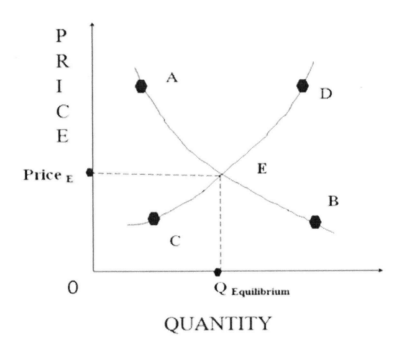

QUANTITY

In a free market system, products seek equilibrium conditions.

The Supply and Demand Curve model just displayed uses gentle curves to represent the Supply function and the Demand function. Some models simply straighten out those gentle curves and use straight lines. Straight lines or curves work equally well for demonstrating the concept of supply and demand.

In the real world, the shapes of supply curves and demand curves are almost never truly known. If the supply functions and demand functions represented by the curves were well defined and well known, many decisions would be easily made. However, the actual functions are only vaguely known, so most decisions about buying and selling include estimations in addition to actual data. There is room for "art" as one makes decisions about buying and selling. The model helps by providing a sound concept. Then real people have to apply the concept to the real world.

In a perfect free market, all potential buyers and all potential sellers would instantly know about the prices and quantities offered by others. Additional suppliers could instantly enter the market or leave the market at no cost. Equilibrium would be achieved instantly, and a new equilibrium point would instantly develop in response to pressures or events outside the market for the product.

Perfection, of course, does not exist. (It comes pretty close when you look at the market for foreign currencies.)

There is almost always some lag in information flows and some cost to enter or leave a market as a supplier. Still, the model works very well and explains real-world price movements and market shifts. A sound grip on the concept of Supply and Demand is a critical asset for anyone who is involved in buying and selling.

Changes to "The Market": All sorts of things can change the market for a product or a service. The invention of the "horseless carriage" dramatically altered the demand functions for buggy whips and for oil. The attack on Pearl Harbor and the United States' subsequent entry into World War Two substantially altered the supply function for labor. Smaller events also have an impact on the supply and demand functions.

The following section shows how the supply and demand model demonstrates the market's response to changes.

Let's start by considering what happens to a shift in the Demand function. The sketch below shows the market for "widgets", (an economist's favorite hypothetical product.) Notice that the market is in equilibrium with an equilibrium price of P sub E One. At that price, Q sub E One widgets are demanded and supplied.

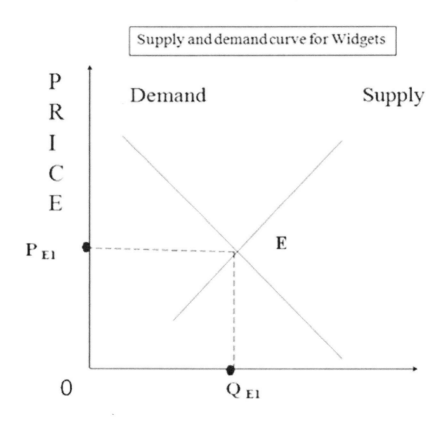

Supply and demand curve for Widgets

Imagine that something has happened to cause Widgets to become more desirable. (Perhaps a new use was discovered for Widgets, or perhaps they became fashionable.) This would create a shift in the demand function as shown below. At the new equilibrium point, more widgets are consumed at a higher price.

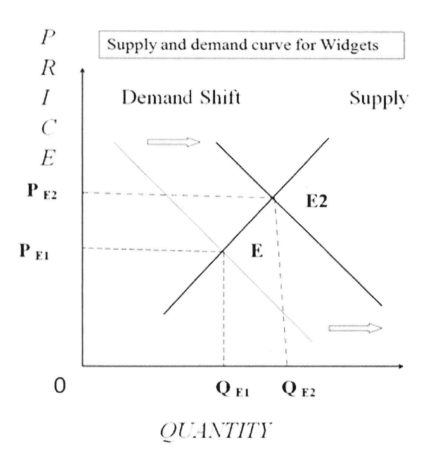

Now let's consider what happens if supply increases. (The supply function can increase for a variety of reasons. More efficient production methods, reduced taxes, reduced regulatory costs or reduced costs of materials and energy could increase supply.) Notice the supply function changes, and a new equilibrium is reached. Prices for Widgets decline, and more are consumed.

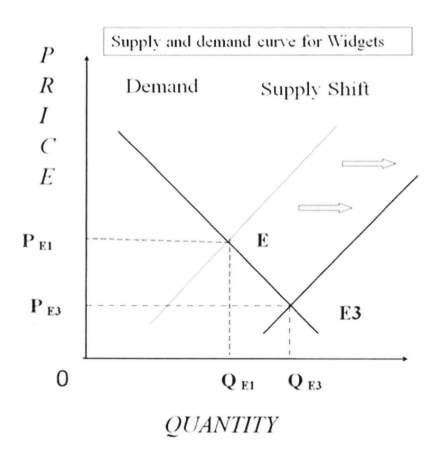

Micro-Economics

The study of economics is usually broken into segments. One segment is called "micro-economics." This is the study of economics as seen by a single business. It is concerned with maximizing profit by finding the most efficient level of production and sales for a given product or service. Multiple factors are examined, such as the source and control of costs, the effects of uncertainty, risk and time, the wisest way to raise capital, etc.

Key terms include: Equilibrium point, price, cost, capital, marginal (as in "marginal revenue, marginal cost and marginal profit"), revenue, profit, supply, demand, fixed costs, variable costs, monopoly, competition.

Macro-Economics

Macro-Economics is the study of the economy from the perspective of a country. It considers unemployment, inflation, investment, interest rates, and growth.

Key terms include: Fiscal policy, monetary policy, interest, inflation, savings, investment, GNP, GDP, unemployment, employment, deflation, growth, recession and depression.

The Macroeconomic Cycle: Understanding the economy of a single business or organization is challenging. Attempting to understand something as complex as the economy of an entire country is even more challenging.

The Macroeconomic cycle is a way to help understand the inter-relationship of a large variety of factors in a national economy.

A simple view of the Macroeconomic cycle begins with the concepts of markets, consumers and businesses. Consumers of goods and services "go to markets" to purchase what they require. Businesses also go to those markets to offer the goods and services consumers require. So, one can start to build a sketch of the Macroeconomic cycle by showing products (and services) being provided to markets by businesses and being provided to consumers from the markets. Of course, consumers have to buy the products and services, so consumers bring money (Consumer Spending, called "C") to markets to pay for the goods and services. Businesses sell the products and services at the markets and bring revenue back to the businesses. (The total revenue of all goods and services is, simplistically, the Gross Domestic Product, GDP. At this stage in the model building GDP = C.)

Businesses need labor in order to provide the goods and services. The go to labor markets to hire the labor. The consumers offer their labor in those markets in order to earn wages and salaries. Adding this concept to the sketch produces the diagram on the next page. (Note the two cycles. One moves clockwise and the other moves counter clockwise.)

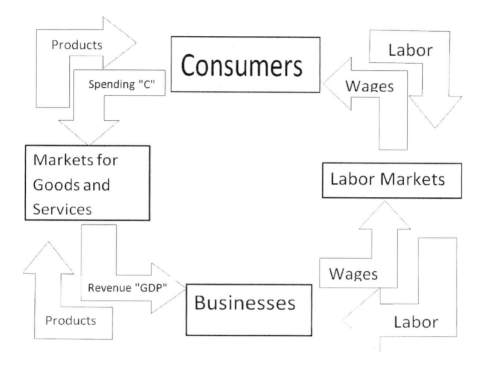

The Start of the Macroeconomic Cycle

Products

Consumers

Labor

Spending "C"

Wages

Markets for
Goods and
Services

Labor Markets

Wages

Revenue "GDP"

Businesses

Products

Labor

At this point, we should start to add some detail.
"Consumers" buy finished goods and services. A
business can sometimes be thought of as a consumer.

In addition, businesses don't just hire labor, they purchase
all sorts of "factors of production", so we can expand
"labor markets" into a "factor markets" or "resource
markets."

19

We should recognize the role of government in the cycle.
Governments also consume goods and services.
Therefore, the simple model adds an arrow for
government spending, "G" , which, along with "C",
represents spending for goods and services. (This
spending all contributes to GDP. GDP =C +G.)

Governments pay for those goods and services by
imposing taxes.

Notice that govenrment spending, in this model, is still
consumption, but with different decision-makers.

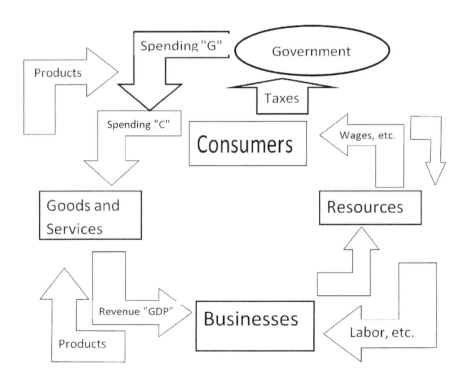

As cluttered as the figure has become, there is still more room for useful complexity.

We need to consider the role of saving, "S", and investment, "I." Consumers do not spend all that they earn. They save some money in banks and other financial institutions. Those banks lend the money to people who want to use it to invest in new businesses, new homes, etc. We could add a box to the chart, call it financial intitutions, and show that consumer savings go into it while businesses borrow from it. The businesses take the money to the products and services market to spend their investment money on what they need. After adding the financial markets, savings and investments to the model, we see that GDP = C + G + I.

There is still more. We haven't yet considered foreign markets. Consumers can divert some of their money into product markets that are in other countries. (We see that diversion as an "import.") Consumers from other countries can bring their money to our product markets. (We see that gain as an "export.") Our GDP is enhanced by exports and diminished by imports.

GDP = C + G + I + Ex

Note that some of C, G, and I, might be spent in foreign markets on imported items. It that case,

GDP = C + G + I + Ex minus Im

The figure below shows a more complex form of the model. As you can imagine, even more complexity can be added, but the model in this form serves well enough for good conceptual reasoning about Macroeconomics.

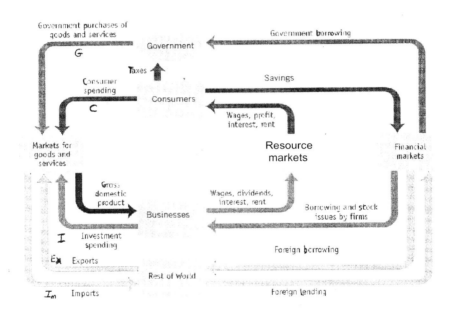

International Economics

When economic activities cross international borders, additional factors have to be studied and understood. One obvious factor is the exchange rates of various currencies. Another significant factor is the differing legal systems. Key terms include: Imports, exports, trade, balance of trade, cartels, tariffs and shipping

Fiscal Policy

Fiscal policy concerns government spending choices (including deficit spending) and government taxation laws.

When the government extracts a dollar in taxes from a tax payer, the tax payer can no longer spend or invest that dollar. In the macroeconomic chart, the "consumer spending" flow and the "private savings/investment" flow will decrease.

When the government spends a dollar, the "government spending" flow increases.

When the amount of government spending is larger than the tax revenues, then the government borrows money. This has an impact on the financial markets and reduces the availability of investment money to other ventures.

See the appendix section on Monetizing the Debt for a discussion of what happens if the government elects not to borrow the money from financial markets and creates it instead.

Monetary Policy

Monetary policy is the set of choices and actions taken concerning the supply of money. (These actions serve to strengthen, diminish or maintain the buying power of the dollar. They are controlled by the Fed – Federal Reserve Board) The four tools of the Fed are:

<u>Open market operations</u> – buying and selling government bonds

If the Fed were to sell government bonds worth $100 million, then $100 million would be absorbed from the money supply. (Instead of $100 million worth of buying power in the system, there would now be $100 million tied up in bonds.) If the Fed were to buy $50 million in bonds, then $50 million in buying power would be added to the system as $50 million worth of bonds are sold to the Fed.

Actions of the US Fed in the years 2010 and 2011 have introduced a dramatic change in the use of open market operations. See the appendix section for a discussion of Monetizing the Debt.

<u>The Reserve Ratio</u> – Setting the legal reserve requirements banks must maintain

Banks hold money from people who deposit money in savings or checking accounts. Banks earn money by lending some of those deposits to other people. The Fed sets a reserve requirement to tell the banks they must keep a certain amount of the deposits on hand. Banks can lend amounts above the reserve requirement. For instance, if the reserve requirement is 10% and a bank has $100 million in deposits, the bank would have to keep $10 million in reserve, and it could lend $90 million. If it were to lend all $90 million, then the money supply would grow by $90 million. A reserve requirement of 12% would reduce the money supply by reducing the amount of money banks can lend.

The Discount Rate – Controlling the interest rate the Fed charges for money it lends to banks.

Banks do business all during the day. At the end of the day, the banks can see if their reserves and cash are adequate or not. If they are not adequate, a bank can borrow the needed reserves from the Fed. The interest on such borrowing is the Discount Rate. If the discount rate is low, banks will be liberal in their willingness to lend money even if they might have to borrow money to maintain their reserves. This would expand the money supply. Conversely, a high discount rate would cause banks to be careful to avoid the need to borrow from the Fed. They would voluntarily keep higher reserves, which would shrink the supply of money.

Term Auction Facility – twice a month auction of cash reserves from the Fed to banks.

The Fed will periodically announce its willingness to extend loans of reserves to banks. The Fed declares the amount to be lent and then allows banks to bid on the interest rate that will be paid. The Fed starts with the highest interest bid and issues the loans until the target dollar amount has been reached. If the Fed sets a high target amount, more banks will "win" their bids for reserves, more reserves will be available in the system, more loans can be made, and the money supply will expand. If the Fed sets a low target or even zero, then banks will not have access to this attractive source of reserves, and loans will shrink causing the money supply to shrink.

More information: This section on monetary tools is, naturally, simplified. You can get more details at http://www.federalreserve.gov/monetarypolicy/fomc.htm

Exercises - Chapter One

1. Ensure you understand the meaning of all "key terms" listed in the section.

2. What happens to the equilibrium quantity and the equilibrium price if supply shrinks? Sketch the shift.

3. What could cause the supply function to diminish? (List at least one natural cause, one "social" cause, and one government action. Be prepared to explain.)

4. What happens to supply curves if business taxes on profits are increased? Why?

5. It is said that business taxes are actually paid by the consumers. Does that make sense or not? Why? (Use your answer to question 4 as a starting point.)

6. Sketch a supply and demand curve for an imaginary product. Assume the government passes a law to freeze the price at the current equilibrium price. Then sketch a curve representing an increase in demand. Compare the new quantity demanded with the new quantity supplied. What will happen to consumers of the product?

Chapter Two – Introductory Political Philosophy

> What is the nature of Man?
> What is the role of government?
> How should government accomplish its role?

The various answers to these three questions shape political philosophies and ideologies. There are many different answers to these questions and many nuances associated with each answer. The answers lead to preferences about which sort of political system is "best", and what sorts of governmental actions are desirable.

For the sake of massive simplicity, let's examine Political Philosophy using the following scale based on the present situation in the USA:

Liberal (Left)  Conservative (Right)

Here is the Liberal (Left) perspective:

American Liberals tend to be worried about the nature of Man. They see individuals as being weak in general. Clever and strong individuals will rise to dominate others. In a free market system, the clever and strong become the capitalists and the owners. While Liberals have reservations about individual capacities in general, they have confidence in the wisdom and merit of specialists, experts and government officials.

American Liberals think government should protect weaker citizens from being dominated by stronger citizens. However, weaker citizens being what they are, that protection requires government to serve as the controlling entity to prevent domination by powerful individuals or corporations. Government is more than just a protector. Government is also a force of positive good. Government, composed of the "best and the brightest", should help the people in just about any way the people wish.

American Liberals tend to be "collectivists". The government is the instrument of the collective will of the people. It is to shape and assist society and sub-groups of society. In the words of President Obama at his inauguration: *"The question we ask today is not whether our government is too big or too small, but whether it works — whether it helps families find jobs at a decent wage, care they can afford, a retirement that is dignified."*

Economic Focus: American Liberals are uncomfortable with Capitalism and Free Markets. They tend to favor government regulation in most cases, and may even be attracted by elements of a command economy.

Simplification: The Left is sometimes described as favoring the "Nanny State." It wants a wise government to care for the people just as a nanny cares for her children. When a problem surfaces, Liberals tend to seek a government solution right away.

Related terms and philosophies: Socialism, Social Democracy -- Marxism and Totalitarianism are at the extreme.

American Liberals and Socialism? American Liberals are sometimes called "socialists". This is technically incorrect as socialists want all the means of production to be owned by the state. It would be more correct to think of American Liberals as "Statists". That is, American Liberals have confidence in the government and would, ideally, see government shape society and its economic activities through the use of government power. "Statism" is a term that is gaining popularity, but it has not been part of the normal set of typical governmental types. Socialism, on the other hand, is a well-known type of government, and its effects are similar to those of statism. Thus, socialism has been used to describe American Liberals as it is the best fit of the common categorizations of government types. Once the term "Statist" becomes more commonly embraced, it would be the better term to describe the type of government favored by American Liberals.

Term Confusion – "Liberal", in its early usage and as it is often used in Europe, means to restrict the power of the State and to applaud the merit of the individual. In the USA, we use the term "Liberal" in the opposite sense. In the USA, a "Liberal " policy often seeks to expand the role and power of government. These contradictory meanings of the word can cause confusion when reading history and when reading political commentary from Europe.

Here is the Conservative (Right) perspective:

American Conservatives acknowledge that Man is flawed. They worry about what happens when a flawed person holds massive power over others. Importantly, American Conservatives believe individuals are best suited to judge their own interests. American Conservatives note that individuals often freely associate to accomplish goals that are beyond the capacity of one individual, and they do so without resorting to the use of coercive power by the government.

American Conservatives recognize that flawed people can prey upon one another. Accordingly, Conservatives require government to protect the lives and property of individuals. Government is to secure our borders, guard us from thieves and murderers, and to do the limited tasks essential to modern living, (such as providing a mechanism to resolve private disputes, maintaining a currency, developing standards and serving as the custodian of public goods.)

American Conservatives recognize that government power is a threat to individual liberty. Governmental power, sovereign power, is exercised by people in government, not by angels. Conservatives want the government to be checked and limited. Government is a "necessary evil" to be watched and contained. As President Washington said: "Government is not reason; it is not eloquent; it is force. Like fire, it is a dangerous servant and a fearful master."

Simplification: Conservatives want government to serve as the "night watchman." It is to build a protective fence to guard us against predators, but, so long as we do not use force to impose our will on others, we should be free to seek our own happiness and prosperity within that fenced area. When a problem surfaces, Conservatives tend to expect individuals or free associations of individuals to find the solution and will turn to government only as a last resort.

Related Terms and Philosophies: Limited government, Laissez-Faire, Libertarianism

Term Confusion: "Conservatives" originally described those who supported the power of the Monarch. In European discourse, a Conservative tends to favor the use of government power to support traditional ends. In the USA, we generally use the term in the opposite sense. A Conservative policy often seeks to restrain the power of the Federal government. These contradictory meanings of the word can cause confusion when reading history and when reading political commentary from Europe.

Goals versus Methods: Modern American political debate is often clouded by the attempt to suggest that the goals of the "other side" are nefarious or flawed or evil. Greater clarity can be gained by focusing on methods rather than goals. For example, people on both the Left and the Right favor good education for children. They share the same broad goal. They differ massively about the best methods to achieve those goals. The same reasoning applies to economic prosperity, health care, national defense, unemployment, and virtually any other subject of national debate. Our discourse will be more effective and useful if we start by finding the shared goal.

The Fringe: There are some very strange ideas to be found on both the Left and the Right. It is tempting to find a bizarre idea from the "other side" and try to assign that idea to everyone on that other side. Avoid that temptation. It is more effective and useful to discuss the clash of ideas represented by the "mainstream views" of the Right or of the Left.

Individual Consistency: It is not uncommon for a politician or leader to favor a Left-wing approach to one situation and a Right-wing approach to another. Our labels for leaders and politicians are useful not because they are absolutes, but because they describe tendencies and preferences. A politician who is a Democrat will generally, but not necessarily always, chose a solution that rests on government power. A politician who is a Republican will generally, but not always, chose a solution that minimizes the role of government and maximizes individual responsibility.

Rights: Any discussion of political philosophy will soon encounter the idea of "rights." These discussions often become tangled because of confusion about the definition of the terms used in the discussion. Please consider the following definitions:

Natural Right - This is a right a person possess simply because he exists. All people have the same natural rights. Natural rights are often said to be God-given rights. A natural right cannot be surrendered by an individual, nor can it justly be taken from an individual.

Right granted by government - A government can declare that a right exists. For instance, the US Constitution declares: "In all criminal prosecutions, the accused shall enjoy the right to a speedy and public trial...."

Entitlements and Claims - Laws passed by governments and contracts created between people often establish obligations and duties. Moral codes also establish sets of duties and obligations. A person may claim he is entitled to something or claim another person or agency is required to perform some act or another. The word "right" is often used to describe someone's legal or moral claim.

Exercises - Chapter Two

1. In "Leviathan", Thomas Hobbes argues that people should submit themselves totally to the absolute rule of a sovereign master, (a king), because otherwise people would find themselves in the State of Nature where life would be "nasty, brutish and short." This statement, while seemingly offering strong support to monarchs, actually contains the seed of the ideas leading to the American Revolution and independence from the monarchy. Explain the assertion about the "seed."

2. The American colonies rebelled against a strong central government. They established a limited and constrained government designed to ensure the protection of individual freedom and Liberty. How has that government evolved? Why?

3. What is the difference between a Democracy and a Republic? Is the difference significant? Why or why not?

4. Liberals and Conservatives have different views about the Nature of Man. Define the two views. Consider what arguments you could offer in support of each perspective or in rebuttal to each perspective. Be prepared to present your ideas.

Chapter Three – Introductory Business Management – The search for Effectiveness and Efficiency

Is our business doing well or poorly?

How well (or how poorly) is it doing?

What can be done to make things better?

Finding answers to questions such as these has been the basis for the evolution of the study of business management. The study applies to "for profit" and to "not-for-profit" organizations. (The primary difference between "for-profit " and "not-for-profit" organizations is that all profits are retained in "not-for-profit" organizations while some profits can be distributed to owners and shareholders in "for-profit" organizations. Both types require good management.)

All businesses need to be concerned with effectiveness and efficiency. A business or a business process is effective if it can accomplish the assigned task. A business or process gains in efficiency when it can accomplish the assigned task with fewer resources. Resources include money (capital), labor, energy, transportation, raw materials, time, etc.

The effort to improve business has come to be divided into several distinct areas of study. Let's examine the following areas: **Strategy, Organization, Finance & Accounting, Operations, Sales &Marketing, HR, IT, Leadership, Decision-making, and Quality.**

Strategy

> What is the purpose of the company or organization?
> How does it propose to accomplish that purpose?
> How will it know if it succeeded or failed?

Most companies start with a relatively clear grip on the first two questions. Over time, they tend to lose sight of the answers. (The answer to the first question tends to degenerate into something like, "to make money", or "to help others.") Far too many companies never get a solid grip on the third question.

It is wise for managers to reflect on these three questions and to ensure they have good, clear answers to them. After that, it is wise to ensure those answers are understood by the other members of the organization.

Strategy plus Organization

An organization ought to start with a solid concept of what it intends to do. Why is it in existence? What are its goals? From that it is a logical step to ask how it expects to accomplish those goals. This is the organization's "strategy." A strategy should be clear and simple, even if it is not easy. As the organization plans how to execute its strategy, it will have to decide what people and resources it will require and how those people and resources should interact. This is called "organization." (Note that "organization" is used in two senses. In one case, "organization means a firm or business or agency, etc. In the other, it means the structure of that firm or business.)

It is vital for an organization to spend time ensuring it has a clear strategy and a compatible structure. These things tend to evolve or drift over time, so a wise manager will review them from time to time.

Finance & Accounting

This area covers several significant issues. The simplest "accounting" functions are to track outbound and inbound flows of money and to be able to know the "bank balance" situation of the company at any time. "Finance" has the task of dealing with capital formation and the management of money, credit, wealth, and debt. A higher order function is called "managerial finance." That means using the cash flows, balances and indicators to evaluate the health of the company, to focus attention on areas that appear to be doing particularly well or particularly poorly, and to find the optimal instruments for holding cash, wealth, credit and debt.

Operations

Operations Management tasks will be different from company to company. In general, however, the Operations Manger will be responsible for making things happen. Here is a list of responsibilities that typically land on the Ops Manager's plate:

38

Inside Sales (Taking orders initiated by customers –
                 Using phone, fax, Internet, etc.)
Inventory Control
Warehouse Operations
Purchasing
Manufacturing/Assembling/Providing the Service
Packaging and Shipping
IT (when not a separate function)
Quality
Training

So, if a function is not clearly part of Sales, Marketing, Finance, HR, Legal, or R&D, it usually winds up in Ops.

Ops places a premium on logic, structure, communication, leadership, and attention to important details. The company car is driving down the street. Ops keeps the engine running and steers the car to keep it in the lane.

Sales & Marketing

Sales and Marketing are related functions that can be combined or handled separately. Both start with an assessment of the "market." (Who wants to buy our product or service? Who might want to buy it? Who else is providing the product or service?) The idea is to forecast the need for the product or service, to figure out where and to whom the product or service can be sold, and to anticipate how much of that product or service our company can expect to sell. (Forecasting is challenging.

Science supports forecasting efforts, but forecasting remains more of an art than a science.)

Marketing deals with knowing the potential customers, their needs, their circumstances, and their preferences. Marketing goes well beyond advertising. Marketing starts with an analysis of the market by considering customers' locations and needs, the competition, and other factors such as laws and regulations. Marketing managers use the market analysis to allow them to consider the "Four P's" of Product, Price, Position, and Promotion. Advertising kicks in when we consider how to make our product or service attractive and when we decide how to inform potential customers about what we have to offer.

Sales encompasses many activities. Sales often includes having a sales representative call on customers in order to help customers meet their needs using the products or services our company provides. At minimum, Sales includes a mechanism to receive orders from customers for the goods or service our company provides. The Sales function often also includes a "customer service" element.

Human Resources

Companies have to deal with multiple administrative tasks. The "human resources department" typically handles the regulatory and legal requirements associated with having employees. In addition, HR finds new employees, trains employees, helps to set pay and benefit scales, provides an avenue of complaint or redress, maintains personnel policies and procedures, maintains the paths for advancement and promotion, maintains disciplinary paths and records, etc. Sometimes the HR department also handles pay and benefits.

Information Technology

IT is an area that is growing in importance. IT includes everything from providing phones, common office computers and Email to running highly complex Enterprise Resource Planning (ERP) systems.

IT is fascinating. That means it can get out of control. From a business perspective, we probably do not want to be out on the "bleeding edge" of technological advancement. We want to remember that we are using the flow of information or the flow of commands and controls in order to accomplish clearly stated goals. The "Information Age" has created extraordinary opportunities, but it has also created pitfalls. Our IT department is to help us enjoy the benefits while avoiding the pitfalls.

Leadership

Leadership is a seemingly simple skill. It means defining and communicating what the organization is to do and inspiring the people to do it. Of course, that is actually quite hard to accomplish. There is much art involved in being an effective leader, and there is a substantial amount of "science" as well. It is an area full of ideas, theories and studies. I will offer you just a few simple leadership rules that might help you.

> Define the goal as clearly and simply as you can.

> Communicate it frequently.

>Take the tough jobs yourself. Lead from the front.

> Be honest. Never lie. Your followers may excuse you for making errors, but they will never trust you again once you lie to them or trick them.

> Accent the positive. Compliment good work and strong effort. Punishment or harsh criticism merely discourages poor behavior. Praise encourages behavior and effort that go beyond the minimum. Besides, people enjoy working in a positive environment.

Decision making

Decisions get made, or not, one way or another. Many theorists recognize the huge advantage one could gain by making even a marginal improvement in the quality of decision making. Accordingly, there are many theories about how we can improve our decision making styles and approaches. Please do not try to chase the latest decision making fads. Instead, look at each new theory you encounter and adopt what seems valuable to you. Look at the outcomes of your decisions. Evaluate the quality of your decision making. Learn from your mistakes and learn from your successes.

It is also important to recognize types of decisions. Some decisions are small, (of little consequence), such as the decision about the type of file cabinet to purchase for one office. Other decisions, of course, can be major, such as the decision about where to build a new facility. Obviously, we want to spend our precious attention units and time on the significant decisions.

Decisions can deal with "one-off" (one time) situations, or they can be deal with systemic or repeated matters. One-off situations simply require solutions that work. Situations that are likely to be repeated merit additional attention. The chosen solution for a repeating situation must not only work, it must work in a way that will permit it to be converted into a normal business practice that can be taught to the staff and followed.

Finally, decision-making is an art. Yes, we can support our decision-making with good numbers-crunching and scientific analysis, but we always face some degree of uncertainty. (Some poor managers like to use that uncertainty as an excuse to avoid rigorous analysis. Better managers use the rigorous analysis and combine it with subjective assessments.) Because of the uncertainty, some of our decisions will have bad outcomes. We should plan on that. Once you have made a decision and are ready to implement it, ask yourself questions such as:

>How will I know the decision was a good one?
>How will I know if the implementation is working or not?
>What are my fallback options?
>What should trigger the use of a fallback option?

Quality

Quality is sometimes a part of Operations. Sometimes it is a separate organization. Quality used to mean checking products before they were sold to ensure the products meet the standards. Now quality usually means developing a system to prevent failures in the first place and to create conditions for "continuous improvement." You will hear about quality management systems such as TQM (total quality management) or "Six Sigma." These quality systems are designed to help a company efficiently provide what it promises to provide.

Language can sometimes create confusion, and it certainly does in the case of quality. "Quality" has a common meaning. It means something that is better or finer. "Quality" also has a specialized meaning in business jargon. In business jargon, "quality" means being within tolerances, meeting the standards, or compliance and assurance of compliance with defined systems. (Please note that the jargon is evolving, and "quality" will almost certainly pick up a few more meanings. That is the nature of jargon.)

A disposable tablecloth that is of low quality in common terms could well be considered of high quality in business jargon because it meets its specifications perfectly. A very fine, precisely made, specialized brass fitting might be considered a quality failure in business terms because the manufacturing process took two extra days.

Quality is concerned with both effectiveness and efficiency. A process must first be tested to see if the outcome meets the standard (effectiveness). Then quality processes seek to find ways to remain effective while employing fewer resources such as time, money and materials (efficiency).

Most quality processes recognize the value that can be gained by involving the whole staff in the search for improvement. Excellent ideas are often generated from within through the use of "quality circles" or other mechanisms to ask employees to look for ways to generate improvements.

Exercise Questions - Chapter three

1. What is the meaning of "effectiveness"?

2. What is the meaning of "efficiency"?

3. What is the business meaning of "quality"?

4. Who establishes an organization's strategy, and what does a strategy do for an organization?

5. What is the difference between Accounting and Managerial finance?

6. How does business management differ when it is employed in a "not for profit" organization as opposed to a "for profit" organization?

7. How does business management differ when it is employed in a government organization as opposed to a business? (Hint: Remember your study of government. consider the source of revenue and the budget process.)

Chapter Four: – American Government and Politics

Most readers will have studied American Government and will have had the opportunity to learn the mechanisms, structures and practices of the US federal government and of state governments. This book assumes you have a good foundation about those matters.

Prior to the American Revolution, with the symbolic, but minor, exceptions of the Athenian city-state and the oligarchy/democracy of Rome, humans were always ruled by a central authority. The leader might have been a chief, a warlord, a king, an emperor, a czar, or a sultan. (In fact, the full list of names for the person in charge is quite impressive.) The ruler might have held power because of strength or birth or, frequently, both. The ruler might have been benevolent or horrid. Whatever the details might have been, the common theme was one of subjugation of the ruled by the ruler.

It seemed to be the "natural order of things" that the strong and capable should hold power over the weaker or less capable. This natural order solidified into control by castes, families, nobles, etc. Those with power strove to keep it or to expand it. Commoners, serfs and other "ordinary folk" had little or nothing to say about how their societies, tribes, nations or countries were to be ruled.

This "natural order of things" did not go unchallenged. Contrary ideas circulated. The total power of sovereigns was challenged. The ideal of Athenian democracy tantalized and motivated many political thinkers.

Additionally, ideas took root concerning "natural rights" and the value of the individual. In the 18th Century, these "radical" ideas finally took form with the establishment of Independence for the American colonies and the birth of the United States of America.

How odd it must have been to imagine that "the masses", "the great unwashed", the uneducated common men, might actually have the final say about how they were ruled. Only the most starry-eyed thought a pure democracy could ever work, but even the somewhat less extreme notion of a representative democracy with leaders selected by the voters was stunningly radical.

The Founders of the USA knew they were embarked upon a grand experiment; the outcome of which was far from certain. One of their first tasks was to prevent the whole thing from falling into the clutches of an ambitious leader. After all, kings and dynasties had risen and fallen throughout history. All that was required to change rulers was for a strong man to rise and to seize the power he craved. What was to prevent the same thing from happening in the fledgling USA? Using ideas from Montesquieu, Locke and others, The Founders devised a system of "separation of powers" and "checks and balances" to create a structure of government that relied on the self-interest of men rather than the Nobility of Man to ensure Liberty and Equality.

The Founders also worried about the unchecked powers of a democracy. A majority can trample on rights just as a tyrant can. Accordingly, the Founders created a rule of law with a Constitutional basis. Majority rule was also checked and limited. Law and rights should restrain and restrict the passions of a majority.

There is a wonderful story that tells of a woman who approached Benjamin Franklin after the conclusion of the Constitutional Convention to ask, "Sir, what form of government have you given us?"

His thought- provoking reply was, "A republic, madam, if you can keep it."

Of course, the dominant feature of a republic is the fact that the power of government is limited by some root law. In our case, it is the power of the Constitution to limit our government's actions that causes the USA to be a republic.

The Constitution is a special document because it limits the power of government. Read the Bill of Rights. (See the Appendix Section.) You will see it does not really emphasize individual rights. Rather, it restricts the power of government.

Are we to keep our republic?

Franklin's concern that the republic might be hard to keep was not frivolous. The former colonies had much in common, but even more differences. Factions were powerful forces in that day, just as they are today. "Liberty", "Equality", and even the word "Republic" itself were imperfectly understood. The French Revolution, which stood on ideas and ideals virtually identical to those that gave birth to the American Revolution, proved how fragile a republic could be as it descended into mob rule, The Terror, and ultimately, a return to rule by a single king or emperor.

Of course, kings and emperors are not the only ones who can exercise unlimited government power. An unlimited democracy (either a representative democracy or a pure democracy) or a dictatorship also exercise total power.

The fate of the Republic is in the hands of its citizens.

Exercise Questions - Chapter Four

(You will have to go beyond this text to answer these questions.)

1. Please identify the following terms:

Liberty
Equality
Republic
Democracy
Faction
Checks and Balances
Separation of Powers (two forms in the US Constitution)
Suffrage
Representative Democracy
Enumerated Powers (general definition)
Elastic Clause
Bill of Rights
Authoritarianism
Totalitarianism

2. Explain why it might be more accurate to call the Bill of Rights, the Bill of Limitations

3. What is the purpose of the 10th Amendment?

4. List the major enumerated powers of the Federal government.

5. Briefly define the processes for amending the Constitution.

6. Distinguish between equality of opportunity and equality of outcome.

7. What was Dr. Franklin worried about? (How might we fail to keep our republic?)

8. Be prepared to discuss Liberty, Freedom and Equality.

9. Briefly describe how the budget for the US government is established.

Chapter Five: Society

We do not really know how society works.

The study of groups of people is one of the topics that falls into the broad area of "Social Science."

The "Social Sciences" are relatively new creations in the academic world, but the study of groups of people has been around for a very long time. It is frustrating to try to understand an individual or a group, but the obvious importance of understanding how people behave continuously inspires efforts to come to grips with the matter.

Much of the traditional effort to understand the actions of people as social creatures, that is, the actions of people as members of groups, consists of observation, speculation and reasoned argument. (The works of Aristotle and Plato demonstrate this exceptionally well.) Unfortunately, debates about society and politics do not lead to a single, convincing set of conclusions. Instead, the debates tend to be endless and inconclusive.

The studies of natural sciences, such as physics and chemistry, on the other hand, have advanced rapidly through the application of the scientific method to the study of natural phenomena. The term "Social Sciences" grew from a speculation that one could, perhaps, use the scientific method to advance our understanding of social phenomena as well. Perhaps scientific rigor could be more broadly applied. Perhaps there is a place for "Social Sciences" that can move beyond philosophy and debate.

Unlike natural sciences, any effort to apply "science" to the understanding of individuals or groups quickly runs into the vexing problem of variation. In natural sciences, we can recreate situations again and again. We can alter a single element and see what effect it has. Our scientific method depends on that level of control and repeatability. Obviously, the scientific method that has worked so well in the natural sciences just doesn't apply to many situations dealing with people and groups of people. Even so, the success of the scientific method in the natural sciences makes it tempting to try to apply its principles, at least to a degree, to the study of social interactions.

These days, the study of people as social creatures, the study of "society", continues along two tracks. The traditional approach of reasoned debate remains active, and the effort to apply the rigor of the scientific method enjoys serious support as well. Our understanding of society remains thin, and we hope our efforts along both lines of study will help us expand our understanding.

What do we know, or think we know, about society?

The study of society is varied and untamed. Ideas abound, and little is certain.

One of the first issues is the question of defining the group of people who will be studied as a "society." Some studies and ideas concern small groups, such as families, teams, or companies. Some studies draw large boundaries and seek to study large groupings such as nations or women or men. Obviously, there are intermediate groupings as well.

Once a student of society has defined a group, the task of studying the group has only just begun. What is to be examined? Here again, the variety is huge. Power structures, authority, laws, customs, mobility, change, expectations, cultures and stereotypes are common elements of study.

As this book addresses "Business and Public Policy", one can limit the questions and ideas about society to those that pertain to business and government.

Society as a "mass"
or
Society as a "collection of individuals"

We can think about society as a collection of individuals or as a mass. The perspective we use will generate substantially different ideas about actions and choices related to business or to public policy.

Naturally, there is really no such thing as "mass society." People are individuals. Each individual makes choices and behaves in accordance with his values and perceptions. That said, it is also clear that individuals respond to pressures from others or perceptions about the attitudes of others. Accordingly, we have a wonderfully

55

muddled tangle when we try to understand large numbers of people.

Businesses choose to use both points of view about people and society. Some businesses minimize reliance on "mass" and focus on the individual (or a single customer). In fact, there is an interesting concept called "value disciplines" that includes the notion that some businesses should choose the value discipline of "customer intimacy" which means the business will alter its products or services to meet the needs of an individual customer. (More information about value disciplines can be found in the Harvard Business Review article, "Customer Intimacy and Other Value Disciplines" by Wiersema andTreacy, January 01, 1993.)

Alternatively, and more commonly, many businesses embrace the idea that it is useful to think of people as parts of a "mass." Understand the shared views of the "mass", cater to those views or alter those views, and then enjoy success. (The world of fashion offers multiple examples of this.)

Marketing is a place where concepts about society and preferences play a huge role in business. We evaluate "markets" (which are groups of people) in order to understand needs and wants. We design communication to help individuals in the "market" know about, understand and desire the products and services we offer.

In the arena of Public Policy, we also see how our understanding of the situation and our choices among competing public policy options are influenced by our perception of "society."

One of the dominant divisions in our perceptions of society shows up in political philosophy. Should people be viewed as individuals or should they be seen as components of some collective group of people?

If people are valued as individuals, then one is led to acknowledge that individuals and individual choices are valuable. Conversely, one is led to be wary of choices and mandates imposed "from above."

If people are seen as part of a mass or a collective, then one is led to attempt to identify groups and to derive public policies that focus on perceptions about groups rather than individuals. Expecting government to make decisions and choices on behalf of groups naturally flows from this perspective. At its extreme, this point of view argues that government and society are effectively the same thing, and government is merely the arm or the voice of the People.

In addition to this broad bifurcation of perceptions (people as individuals or people as the mass), some political operatives have found it useful to define and to emphasize smaller sets or groups of people in their quest to influence and gain political power. "Identity Politics" is the term used to describe this effort to classify people into specified sub-groupings and to emphasize membership in those sub-groupings for the purpose of influencing political choices and gaining political power. For example, we see efforts to categorize people as Young or Senior or African-American or Hispanic followed by efforts to appeal to voters on the basis of how policies or political platforms will favor their particular sub-set.

Exercises - Chapter Five

1. What is the relationship between government and society?

2. Does your answer to question one change if you consider society to be a collection of individuals?

3. Does your answer to question one change if you consider society as a mass?

Chapter Six: Public Policy

Public Administration and Public Policy are studied by those who want to understand or assess government decisions and policies, influence government decisions, or create government actions or programs.

The study of Public Policy derives from two major circumstances. The first circumstance occurs when a government official is handed a situation and instructed to go fix it or improve it. The natural questions are: "How?" and "What should be done?" The second circumstance occurs when government has taken an action and people want to evaluate that action. "How well or poorly is the government's action or policy working?"

The study of public policy is complicated because policy is based on a tangle of multiple political motivations as well as serious efforts to understand or to administer a situation effectively. On top of that, the situations being addressed are almost always incredible complex.

The Actors:

"Public Servants": Our government is staffed with a combination of elected or appointed officials and unelected administrators. In broad theory, the elected or appointed officials represent the will of the people and set the direction for government policy and actions. The administrators are intended to be non-political experts who know how to turn the cranks that run government departments. (You might remember from your study of US history how the 'spoils" system resulted in mass firings as newly elected officials cleaned out the people who had been employed by the previous administration and replaced them with members of the victorious party. This system prevented the development of experienced administrators, so we passed the "Civil Service Act" to protect the administrators. Think of it as a sort of "tenure" system.)

"Bureaucrats": Government employees who are acting the way I want them to act are public servants. They are fine fellows who deserve our respect. Government officials who are not acting as I wish are bureaucrats. They are obstructionist, wasteful and lazy. One person's bureaucrat is another person's public servant.

Academicians, Lobbyists, think-tank employees, analysts, and journalists: Many people are interested in the impact of government policies and actions. These people develop proposed policies or evaluate existing policies. They do so across a spectrum of involvement ranging from relatively detached and objective to clearly partisan and manipulative.

All actors apply pressures, formal and informal, to influence the outcome of policy analysis.

The Methods of Analysis:

"Knee-jerk": Knee-jerk analysis is not analysis at all. It is the taking of a reflexive action or position. I include it only because so much of what is presented as analysis is not analysis at all. It is "knee-jerk" analysis or argumentation. While such analysis has little to support it, it is, none-the-less, frequently used and often quite persuasive.

"The Normative Approach": Those using the normative approach have a concept of how things ought to be. They use this as the standard to judge a proposed or existing policy. They favor policies that reflect or promote their vision. As M.E. Hawkesworth states in "Theoretical Issues in Policy Analysis", normative policy analysis employs the analyst's values, (which might be things such as "fairness" or "justice" or "redistribution"), to supplement efficiency during the analysis. (Critics of the normative approach might argue it merely provides the appearance of analytical rigor to what is just "knee-jerk" analysis.)

"The Rational Approach": The scientific method paved the way for huge advances. The logic and rigor of the scientific method hold powerful appeal. The social sciences lack the "repeatability" of the hard sciences, so efforts to adapt the scientific method to the social sciences have been frustrating. Still, the appeal is there. Accordingly, social scientists, (and public policy analysts broadly belong in that category), seek a rigorous and "scientific" approach to the analysis of public policy. (The lure of "positivism" is strong.) The rational approach to policy analysis is the result. It requires the analyst to examine public policy using logic, facts, and reason in a clearly defined set of steps. (Careful here. There is no single "rational approach." Academicians love to alter or to modify theories. Accordingly, one could, no doubt, discover a variety of sets of steps to be taken during "rational analysis." I will present a simple set of steps common to most varieties of rational analysis.)

The Steps in the Rational Approach:

>Identify the issue.
>Identify the goals and how to measure them
>Develop several possible paths (alternatives) to the goals
>Evaluate the alternatives. (This is easy to say, but hard to do. Generally, this step will include a cost-benefit analysis and a deliberate effort to anticipate unintended consequences.)
>Choose an alternative
>Implement the alternative. (This step is generally outside of the hands of the analysts, but it is still part of the process.)
>Evaluate the results.

"The Incremental or "Humble" Approach: If you follow all of the steps in the rational approach, you will frequently get to the evaluation stage and say, "Rats! We didn't really hit the target." So, the process starts over as you try to steer the outcomes of the policy closer to the goal. The Incremental Approach argues that such a situation is to be expected. Large and complex policy issues are just plain beyond our ability to "solve" correctly with one iteration of the rational approach. Accordingly, proponents of the

Incremental Approach favor taking small steps followed by adjustments to those steps as one seeks to reach the goals. It is a deliberately "humble" approach in that it recognizes we are not able to create a fully effective policy right at the start. The approach values pilot programs and respects the advantage that we enjoy in the USA because our states often employ a variety of different approaches to solve similar problems.

Exercises - Chapter Six

1. The last step in "the rational approach" is to evaluate the results. Why is that important?

2. What is meant by "cost-benefit analysis"?

3. Philip Howard wrote "The Death of Common Sense" which includes many examples of public officials behaving and choosing in ways that defy common sense and reasoning. How is it that our public policies could generate so many examples of "cement-headedness" and ineffectiveness?

4, What is the role of politics in the formulation of public policies?

Chapter 7 - Economic and Social Revolutions: The Dawn of the Automation Revolution

Human economic , social and political conditions change over time.   This chapter considers the broad history of such changes and speculates about future developments.

Early humans were hunters and gatherers who lived in family bands and tribes. In spite of certain idealized images of the romantic life and virtues of "noble savages", life based on hunting and gathering was harsh and short. Almost every waking hour had to be devoted to scraping out a bare existence.

The Farming and Herding Period

Early humans finally transitioned out of hunting and gathering into farming and herding. That transition radically altered life for people.

The most obvious economic change was a major improvement in "productivity". Under conditions of farming and herding, rather than hunting and gathering, people could meet the requirements of survival and existence with fewer manhours. The "surplus" time or labor could be put to other uses. Specialization became possible.

Of course, the transition to farming, (in particular), also implied additional security needs. Unlike bands of hunters and gatherers who can simply move away from a threat or a depleted zone, farmers are tied to the soil. Security requirements grew. Land had to be possessed and protected. Crops had to be harvested and stored. People developed a sense of permanence and a longer time horizon. Tribes, figuratively, took root and grew into a variety of societies ruled by the "strong right arm" of the leader.

Over time, people learned to farm better and to herd better. Productivity gradually improved. Crafts evolved. Sciences, religion, philosophy and warfare evolved. Specialization continued to develop, and communities became more complex. Power was still exercised by the strong, although rulers began to buttress their claims to power by calling on the support of religion and bloodline.

The farming and herding period endured for centuries. Clever and resourceful people invented remarkable improvements offering better and better productivity, but economic activity was fundamentally limited by sources of physical power. Human labor, augmented by the labor of domesticated animals, such as horses and oxen, was required for almost everything. Mills powered by waterwheels, and the rare windmill, offered significant improvements in specific geographic areas, but physical power limitations constrained economic improvement.

All of these economic changes generated corresponding social changes. Farmers and herders developed societies with more specialization and stability than the societies common to hunters and gatherers. People developed more and varied distinctions about the status, place, duties, responsibilities and power of individuals or groups.

The Industrial Revolution

The Eighteenth Century and Nineteenth Century were radically transformational. The invention of a practical and powerful steam engine allowed people to benefit from a major improvement in power output. Significantly, a steam engine could generate power almost anywhere, and it could even power transportation devices such as locomotives and ships. The massive improvement in power opened the door to stunning improvements in productivity associated with mining, milling, iron, steel, and machine tools. Railroads and canals permitted faster and cheaper transportation of people, goods and materials.

Even more productive doors were opened by the invention of electric engines and internal combustion engines. Creative humans rapidly developed innovative ways to employ the new power sources and associated inventions. Productivity and inventiveness surged. Machines permitted amazing improvements in agriculture, metallurgy and textiles. Each farmer could now feed many more people than before. Each craftsman could now generate more and better goods per day.

Later, Henry Ford's use of large scale standardization and mass production techniques accelerated the economic productivity of each person; opening the door to even more inventiveness and growth.

The Industrial Revolution dramatically increased specialization and concentrated large numbers of people in towns and cities. While people's needs could be met more and more easily, people's wants expanded. Change was rapid enough to be unsettling. Sons and daughters no longer expected to live lives virtually identical to the lives of their parents and grandparents. Contact was no longer limited to the handful of people within walking distance of the farm. (As an aside, we can see an accelerated version of this social transformation in China today. The Chinese government has permitted an increase in economic liberty. The result is an explosion of activity and a rush to the cities by those who are allowed to leave the countryside. The economic changes have dramatically altered the social landscape. How those changes will play out remains to be seen.)

The Age of Liberty

The Eighteenth and Nineteenth centuries were remarkable for more than their stunning improvements in economic output and inventiveness. People also created radical new views about individuals and government. Prior to the Eighteenth Century, people had always been ruled by the strong. Chiefs, Kings, Khans, Emperors, Tsars and their associated dynasties rested on foundations of strength. Leaders ruled because they had the strength to do so. That idea was challenged by the rise of Classic Liberalism.

Classic Liberal ideas, (not to be confused with the modern American use of the word "Liberal"), emphasized natural rights and the value of each individual. Legitimate government came not from mere power but from the consent of the governed and from respect for Natural Law. The American Revolution began a grand experiment with the idea of limited government and natural individual rights. The experiment also includes the notion of democratic choice, but it rejects Democracy (pure or representative) in favor of Rule of Law as established in constitutionally based Republics.

The Rise of Capitalism

The replacement of monarchies with republics (or with the equivalent "Constitutional Monarchies") introduced two key concepts that serve as the foundation for the rise of Capitalism. The first concept is the right to own property. The second is the stability inherent in "rule of Law". Once individuals had a reasonable expectation they could own and employ their property as they saw fit, and once they came to believe the fruits of their labors would not be plundered by rulers or neighbors, Capitalism could develop. Creative energies were unleashed. Invention and efficiency emerged from thousands of minds. Adam Smith's "invisible hand" of the free market-place led to the most efficient allocation of scarce resources in the service of vast numbers of individual wants and needs. The rich economic growth of the Industrial Revolution and beyond is fueled by self-interested individuals seeking to improve their situations secure in the knowledge their property and such wealth as they may generate will be safe from plunder.

The Information Age and Rate of Learning

How did people acquire the knowledge to transform their societies and economies over time? What will allow people to generate more advances now and in the future? Pause for a moment to consider how human knowledge and understanding grows.

A hunter might figure out the behavior patterns of deer herds in his area. That hunter can pass his knowledge to other hunters in his band. Over time, as a result of the slow and intermittent contacts between bands, that knowledge can gradually spread to other hunters in other bands. One of those hunters could apply the knowledge a bit differently and gain a new insight leading to another step forward in the ability to hunt.

A farmer might develop a particularly valuable technique for clearing land. That technique can be shared with other farmers in the area. Again, through the slow and intermittent contact between communities, knowledge can spread, insights can grow, and abilities can improve.

Craftsmen took on apprentices who learned the hard-won techniques of their masters. Every so often, a craftsman would gain an insight that led to an improvement. Slowly, the improvement would spread.

Human knowledge and abilities expand in fits and starts as individuals see what others have done and, in turn, generate a new insight or a different application. We rely on the foundation of earlier insights to generate new ones. We see a cycle of "insight - sharing of insight - new insight". As Sir Isaac Newton said in response to the praises for his great contributions to Physics, "if I have seen farther than others, it is because I stood on the shoulders of giants."

Consider how the invention of writing can influence this process of learning, sharing and learning some more. With writing, information can be kept and stored. It can be shared more widely, and it can endure over time. Accordingly, the cycle of insight, sharing, and new insight can happen more frequently, and we can learn more in a shorter period of time.

The invention of the printing press offered dramatic improvements to the learning cycle. The average time required to commit something to writing was slashed. Many copies of information could be created and widely spread.

As printing became more and more efficient, people were able to print journals and periodicals in addition to books. This change led to a remarkable acceleration of the growth of knowledge. In a short time cycle, a matter of mere months, an idea could be shared, considered by others and refined.

Jump from the printing press to the Internet. Today, the Internet permits ideas to be broadcast, considered by huge numbers of people, critiqued and refined all in a matter of hours or minutes. The "insight, sharing, new insight" cycle has been compressed to a remarkably short period, and the extent of the spread of an idea is almost without limit. The new "Information Age" has accelerated the growth of knowledge to stunning levels.

What of the future? Where is this accelerating growth of knowledge leading?   Let's consider possible changes in economics, society and government.

The Automation Age

The Economic Future of The Automation Age

The jump to farming & herding from hunting & gathering was revolutionary. Production radically advanced. People reorganized their social and political structures. The jump beyond that caused by the Industrial revolution was also revolutionary.   Now, we are now at the border of a new revolutionary jump as we enter the Automation Age.

The age we are leaving, the mature industrial age, was made possible by the invention of remarkable new power sources, both fixed and mobile. The new power sources allowed people to do things never before possible and to produce at previously unthinkable rates. Similarly, the doors to the new age, the Automation Age, are computer technology and engineering technology changes that allow people to do things never before possible.

Advancements in sensing technology and machine design permit machines to perform tasks quickly and precisely. Computer technology permits people to control machines. Purely from the perspective of productivity, fewer and fewer manhours are required to produce goods. Additionally, and significantly, engineering advances now allow the accomplishment of tasks never before possible.

71

Miniaturization, "nanotechnology", powerful communication networks and other advances make possible the invention of new products and new capacities.

Automated machines and robots perform a wide array of tasks. As those in the robotics and automation fields often say, automated machines are particularly useful for doing tasks that are "dirty, dull, difficult or dangerous". Automated machines can operate in toxic or uncomfortable environments. They will quickly, accurately and repetitiously perform tasks. They can, with specialized sensing, shaping, and power applications, do things humans cannot do well or cannot do at all. They allow tasks to be performed without putting people at risk. The range of tasks and activities performed by automated machines is large and growing at an accelerating rate.

The waves of new products and capabilities coupled with leaps in efficiency in the production of existing products mark a new economic revolution with effects that will be as transformative as the effects of the earlier revolutions. While no one can predict the details of the new developments, we can be certain our economic circumstances will permit basic human needs to be met with fewer and fewer required manhours.

The Social Future of the Automation Age

When economic revolutions improve productivity, fewer
manhours are required to produce basic needs or wants.
More time is freed for specialization or leisure. The
automation age is already demonstrating this effect.
("Industrial farming" methods coupled with automated food
processing and more efficient logistics mean one person
can farm in the USA while 99 people do something else.
While this effect is most pronounced in industrialized
countries, the capability is spreading.) As it is with the
production of food, so it is with the production of many
other goods. Automated machines grouped into
automated factories can produce large volumes of
products and require few workers beyond a set of control
specialists and maintenance teams. (The new term, "dark
factories", has been coined to suggest these factories
require so few people that lights are not even needed in
the work spaces.)

The implications are fascinating. As the number of
manhours required to sustain life shrink, starvation and
absolute poverty will no longer threaten people as they
once did. (This condition has already been achieved in
the USA and in other industrialized nations, and it can
spread throughout the globe.) The average person will
enjoy greater and greater control over materiel aspects of
his life. Specialization will become more possible and
more necessary. Thinking, learning, communicating and
cooperating will become the key skills people must
master. Fewer requirements will exist for people who can

73

merely perform manual labor. What social arrangements will follow from such a situation?

Just as the new economic conditions of the Industrial Revolution invoked changes in the social structure of the farming and herding communities, so will the new economic conditions of the Automation Age generate changes in today's social structures. While it is too early to anticipate the full scope of those social changes, one can speculate.

Start with the recognition that automation capabilities coupled with powerful and reliable communication capacities eliminate the need to concentrate workers near factories and large offices. Removing the imperative to concentrate workers opens the door to the possibility of dispersal. Will substantial numbers of people leave the densely populated areas?

Continue with the recognition that the automation era puts a premium on skilled technicians, creative engineers, competent managers and resourceful entrepreneurs. How will educational systems evolve to meet the needs of the era? What implications does an automation age hold for the set of people who are well below average in ability or willingness to learn?

Societies shape themselves to accommodate the cultural conditions, economic conditions, and power realities they face. (Of course, all of those things interact and change over time.) The advent of the age of automation means societies will have to adjust to dramatic improvements in

74

productive efficiency as well as the rapid development of new products and capacities. People will confront changes at rates they have never before had to handle.

While I cannot predict how societies will seek to adapt, I can safely predict each adaptation will endure only briefly (in the scale of social change) before additional adaptations will be required.

The Political Implications of the Automation Age

The Automation Age brings stunning economic advances. Those economic advances will set the stage for potential social changes. One can anticipate political changes will also follow. What political changes might one anticipate?

In order to speculate about future political structures, one should first develop general thoughts about the impact of the coming economic and social changes.

Consider the impact of automation in an industrialized nation in the key area of "needs and wants". The efficiency of automation will permit a person's absolute needs to be met with ever smaller amounts of resources and skilled labor. At the same time, creative and imaginative people will be generating more and more products and services to enhance consumers' lives. Our "wants" will be dramatically expanding.

Consider the impact of automation in an industrialized nation in the key area of required skills. Energetic and competent people will be valuable participants in the economy. They will be able to earn a comfortable living. People who can only offer manual labor will be competing against more efficient machines should they seek employment in the industrial sectors. Accordingly, people with limited skills will find few jobs relative to their numbers, and those jobs will be confined to service sectors not well suited to automation. One can predict many people with limited capacities and minimal skills will have difficulty finding work at all, and will earn only low wages when they can find work. Although their absolute needs will probably be met (through some combination of wages, welfare and charity), they will have frustratingly limited means to satisfy their wants.

Given this set of conditions, what sorts of political structures and pressures will the future bring?

Speculation About the Political Conditions

As previously stated, the Age of Automation creates dramatic new circumstances. Automated machines plus anticipated new developments in science, technology and invention will have "conquered" absolute poverty by making it possible to provide the necessities of life with modest costs in resources and manhours. However, while true "needs" will be generally easy to meet, "wants" will have multiplied, and, although many people will be able to satisfy a large number of "wants", there will be significant pressures to find ways to satisfy even more "wants". At the same time, unskilled manual labor will be less valuable. People who can bring little to the economic marketplace beyond unskilled labor will face significant frustrations as they match their limited earning power against the costs of their materiel desires.

I must emphasize how unusual these new pressures are compared to the pressures people have typically faced throughout history and compared to the pressures faced by many people who do not live in industrialized countries. Life-threatening hunger and poverty have, until recently in the time scale of human development, always been a major factor. While there have always been wants and desires, the compelling pressure of survival established a clear priority. "Wants" are pale things of small matter until "needs" have been met.

However, people living in the conditions created by the automation age give very little thought to "needs". The question is not, "Can we eat?" Instead, the questions are "What shall we eat, and how can we avoid eating too much?" The situation is similar for shelter and clothing. When economic circumstances have advanced far enough to free people from worry about survival, people turn their focus to "wants". However, "wants", unlike "needs", have no definable minimum threshold. There is no limit to economic desires. In fact, we enthusiastically invent new ways to delight, serve and amuse ourselves, so the menu of "wants" is always expanding.

However, resources are required to generate the means to satisfy "wants". Accordingly, "wants" cannot be satisfied for free. Money serves as the shorthand mechanism to allow people to command resources. Those with little or no money might be able to meet their needs, (perhaps with the help of others), but they will be able to satisfy few of their "wants". Those with more money can satisfy more of their "wants".

This line of thinking suggests the existence of a set of people, those who only offer manual labor, who will be marginally equipped to earn material success. While we can reasonably anticipate these people will not face the threat of literal starvation, we can also anticipate they will be "hungry" to satisfy some of their long list of "wants". This set of people, in democratic systems, will provide pools of support for politicians who promise to use the power of the state to redistribute wealth and earnings. (See the rise of Social Democracy in European countries.)

As the government becomes ever more and more involved in economic choices and outcomes, prudent private sector business leaders will seek to influence government actions in their fields. (They may seek influence to prevent damaging governmental actions or to use the power of government to enhance their own prospects.)

Free market Capitalism and the concept of limited government will face political pressures from the mass of marginally skilled citizens as well as from the "Crony Capitalists". President Bill Clinton famously declared "the era of big government is over". The political pressures of the Automation Age may cause his declaration to have been dramatically incorrect. Humankind's experiment with the notions of Liberty and individualism may prove to be brief.

Obviously, this concluding section is highly speculative. I encourage the reader to consider and evaluate the points raised in the section, not to accept them at face value.

Exercises - Chapter Seven

1. the Luddites of the 19th century worried that technological advances would deprive people of work; thereby creating social and human chaos. As it turned out, the Luddites were partially correct. Labor saving machines did replace a great number of manual laborers. However, the Luddites were also partially wrong. The society and economy generated additional demands for workers so the Luddites' fear of a vast pool of unemployed workers failed to materialize. The Age of Automation could revive the Luddite movement as automated machines will surely replace large numbers of simple assembly line workers. Will the Luddite fears of a large pool of unemployed workers be well-founded or not in the Automation Age? Defend your response.

2. Describe the social structures that should evolve from the Automation Age.

3. Consider the following assertion: People living in the Automation Age will not be divided into the "Haves" and "Have Nots", but will, instead, be divided into the "Haves" and "Have Lots". This assertion is based on the expectation that even poor people in the Automation Age will be able to satisfy their needs. (As Dnesh D'Souza* wrote, "I really want to live in a country where the poor people are fat".) Test this argument by investigating the living conditions of poor people in America. Find information about the living conditions of the poorest 5-10% (or some similar group) of Americans in modern times. Compare those living conditions with the middle class of Americans in an earlier period, such as the 1950's or 1960's. (Living conditions would include such things as size of living space, number of bathrooms, ownership of cars, TV, pools, air conditioning, etc.)

   Is it valid to argue even poor Americans now have all of their materiel needs met and are living as comfortably as the middle classes of an earlier time?

* What's So Great About America by Dnesh D'Souza, 2002, Regnery Publishing, Washington DC p77

4. Define "Class Warfare" as a political tool. Find examples of its use.

5. Why would class warfare be a successful political tool?

6. Find at least one example of a country whose government engaged in "economic leveling". Did the policy succeed politically? What were the economic results?

7. In "The Road to Serfdom", F. A. Hayek argues people in democracies will willingly surrender their liberty by voting to give government ever greater powers in exchange for the promise of economic security and ease. Does the argument still apply if virtually all people already have their basic economic needs satisfied?

8. Some pundits see Americans dividing into "Red State" and "Blue State" categories. Do the conditions of the Automation Age reinforce this division or reduce it?

9. As Dr. Benjamin Franklin left Constitution Hall, a woman asked, "Dr. Franklin, what form of government have you given us"? He replied, "A republic, madam, if you can keep it".

   A. What is a republic?

   B. Do the conditions of the Automation Age increase or decrease the challenges associated with "keeping a republic"? Defend your answer.

Appendix Section - Short Essays and Explanations

The health of the American economy is a critical component of business matters, societal matters and public policy choices. At the same time, business, societal and governmental issues all influence the state of the American economy. The interactions are complex, frustrating and significant.

This section illuminates key issues. The essays and explanations serve as a basis for discussion and debate. They are a combination of fact, analysis and opinion.

Appendix A - The Debt Ceiling

in the summer of 2011, the matter of the debt ceiling was a significant political issue. The US government was borrowing money at a massive rate, and it was about to reach the legal debt limit, ($14.3 trillion). The prospect of hitting the debt limit led to political debate, some of which was, unhelpfully, based on the improper linkage of the debt ceiling with "default." Although the debate about the issue receded with the passage of the "Budget Control Act of 2011", the issue is set to regain prominence because the Federal government's deficit spending is pushing total borrowing up against the new debt ceiling of $16.4 trillion. The ceiling should be reached prior to the end of 2012; generating another debate about the crisis of debt.

The issue of the debt ceiling will generate political debate each time borrowing pushes a new debt limit. Each such debate risks being clouded by confusion about some of the terms used in the debate. Accordingly, this appendix provides information about "deficit", "debt" and "default." A clear understanding of these terms should help avoid confusion.

The situation in 2011 serves as a vehicle to explain the terms.

The **debt ceiling** is a legal limit on the amount of money the US government may borrow. That limit is established by law. The idea behind a debt limit is to try to restrain the politicians' natural tendencies to borrow from the future in order to spend in the present. In February 2010, the debt limit was established as $14,294 billion, ($14.3 trillion in rounded terms). (http://www.treasurydirect.gov /govt/charts/charts_debt.htm retrieved 14 June 2011) $14.3 trillion is about $46,300 per citizen or about $185,000 per family of four. $14.3 trillion dollars was almost equal to the gross domestic product which is the total of all goods and services sold in the USA in a year.

The national debt and the annual budget deficit are related but different. The **"deficit"** is the difference between revenue and spending in a given year. (When the federal revenue exceeds federal spending, the US experiences a "surplus" rather than a deficit, a condition that rarely happens.) The **"debt"** is the total of the deficits less the surpluses over the years.

The USA had effectively reached the debt ceiling as of July 2011. The Treasury Department used certain accounting steps to prevent a technical breach of the debt limit, but it could only delay matters by weeks.

Our tax revenues for FY 2011 were projected to be about $2.2 trillion. (FY 2011 means "Fiscal Year 2011." The fiscal year for the USA runs from 1 October 2010 to 30 September 2011.) Spending for FY 2011 was projected to be about $3.7 trillion. Thus, the deficit was projected to be about $1.5 trillion for FY 2011.

Putting this on a monthly basis (which fails to reflect the seasonality of government revenues and spending, but which offers a rough assessment of the situation), the

USA expected monthly revenues to average $185 billion per month while spending averaged $308 billion per month. Therefore, the deficit would average $125 billion per month in round terms.

Throughout history, as the federal government spent more money than it took in as revenue, it borrowed the excess amount it spent. (The government borrows money by selling bonds, or notes or "T-bills" which work much like a corporate bond. The creditor gives the government money in exchange for a bond. The government promises to pay the face value of the bond when it reaches its expiration date.) Borrowing money to pay for deficit spending is legal until the debt ceiling is reached. Once the debt ceiling is reached, the government is not legally permitted to borrow extra money. Accordingly, using figures reflecting the spending and income rates of 2011, once the debt ceiling is reached, the federal government would only be legally permitted to spend the $185 billion per month it receives in revenues. $125 billion of additional intended spending would have to be foregone.

(This is equivalent to a person who earns $2,000 in take home pay each month but who uses a credit card to borrow $1,000 in order to spend $3,000 each month. When the credit card limit is reached, the person still can spend $2,000 a month, but can no longer borrow the extra $1,000. Obviously, that person will have to make some important decisions about how to cut his spending.)

Trying to decide where to cut $125 billion of spending each month was a major task with powerful economic and political consequences. One could avoid that unpleasant task simply by raising the debt ceiling and borrowing more money. Of course, raising the debt ceiling does not resolve the fundamental problem of deficit spending, and it aggravates the difficulty of developing an eventual solution. Even so, raising the debt ceiling is seductive as it allows politicians to dodge the tough choices about how to put our fiscal house in order.

In 2011, the US government chose to postpone the debt ceiling crisis with the "Budget Control Act of 2011." In simplified terms, that act did two things. First, it provided a set of mechanisms that will effectively establish a new debt ceiling of $16.4 trillion. Second, it established a "Super Committee" charged with finding $1.5 trillion in deficit reduction over ten years. An automatic "sequestration" of across the board cuts would kick in should the super committee fail to reach agreement.

http://abcnews.go.com/blogs/politics/2011/07/debt-ceiling-framework-where-they-landed/

The Super Committee could not reach agreement. The political debate about cutting the deficit is heating up as this book goes to press. That debate, and future such debates, will probably include concerns about the debt ceiling. This leads us to consideration of the third term, "default."

Some people worry that failure to raise the debt limit would result in a US **default** on its obligations. In fact, during the debates in 2011, fear of a default was prominently used by those who argued in favor of raising the debt ceiling. The fear is politically powerful, but it is economically incorrect. Failure to raise the debt ceiling need not result in a default. A default would only occur if the USA could not pay back a loan (a treasury bond) as it comes due. Once the debt ceiling is reached, the USA could not add to the amount it has already borrowed, but it could continue to "roll over" existing bonds as they come due. ("Rolling over a bond" means reissuing it to the original creditor with a new expiration date. It could also mean reissuing a bond to a different creditor and paying off the first creditor.) Rolling over a bond merely extends the time frame of a debt. It does not increase the debt.

Appendix B - Monetizing the Debt - USA

"Monetizing the Debt", as used in today's political and economic debates, refers to the practice of borrowing from oneself. It is the modern equivalent of "printing money" with nothing to back it.

Money originally had "intrinsic value." A coin contained metal, and the metal had value. As you learned in economics, money is now just a commonly accepted medium of exchange. A US dollar has no real or intrinsic value. It only has value because people trust that it can be used in the future to exchange for goods or services. That trust is earned, and we say that the value of the dollar is backed by the full faith and credit of the USA.

Experience with notes such as our present dollar, (a "federal reserve note"), teaches that mistrust and inflation can ruin the value of a dollar. Accordingly, the USA established the Federal Reserve Board, the "Fed", and gave it the tasks of controlling the panics on our banking system and of maintaining the value of our money. The current mission of the Fed is "to promote effectively the goals of maximum employment, stable prices, and moderate long-term interest rates."
(http://www.federalreserve.gov/pf/pf.htm.)

"Promoting stable prices" is another way of saying, "fight inflation. Maintain the buying power of the dollar." (The tools available to the Fed are described in the section on Economics.)

One way to control the money supply is through open market operations. Normally, in an open market operation, the Fed would buy or sell US bonds in order to absorb excess dollars from the supply of money (by selling bonds) or to inject additional dollars into the supply of money (by buying bonds). These bonds have, until recently, been originally issued almost the same way corporations issue bonds. If the government or a corporation wants to borrow a million dollars, it offers bonds, and an investor trades money for the bonds.

Recently, the US government has been running astonishing deficits. (They are greater than a trillion dollars each year.) In the normal course of events, in order to spend money beyond the amount of incoming revenue, the government would offer bonds in the financial markets to induce investors (including other countries) to trade their money for US bonds. However, if you flood the market with massive bond offerings, very hefty interest rates would have to be offered to induce investors to buy the bonds. Rather than face huge interest rates, and the corresponding impact such rates would have on the economy as it they drive up the cost of corporate investing, the Fed and the US government are now engaged in **"monetizing the debt."** Rather than having to raise money in the financial markets, the US government trades its bonds to the Fed. The Fed buys the US government bonds, and the US government spends the money.

Where does the Fed get the money to buy the bonds? It just creates it. (That is the "printing press.") In effect, the government is borrowing money from itself. Obviously, that cannot be sustained. Every nation that has tried it has come to monetary and economic grief. (See Weimar Germany post WWI or Argentina in the late 1900s.)

Inflation: One of the problems of monetizing the debt (or "printing money") is the growth of inflation. If more dollars are chasing the same number of goods and services, then the prices of goods and services will increase. Inflation is the increase over time in the price of a product or service. We track the changes in prices through the consumer price index. Inflationary effects are normally reported using a core inflation measure that excludes food prices and energy prices. (Inflation reports are also adjusted for seasonal variation and often restated after more detailed information is collected and absorbed.) As you can imagine, there is some debate about the wisdom of excluding food and energy price changes, but that is what we do.

Inflation rates that exclude food and energy costs are modest at the moment. Will inflation remain modest? You can find people who say yes and people who say no. I am persuaded by the reasoning of those who expect high inflation in the future. The money supply is rising faster than the consumer price index, and it is rising faster than the growth of GDP. That is a prescription for substantial inflation. The inflation has been held in check in part because Americans, worried about the economic future, have responded with caution. They have increased their savings and reduced their spending. That activity can absorb some of the inflationary pressure, but it cannot do so for long. Rising food prices suggest that the "normal" inflation rate will soon reflect the inflation caused by more dollars chasing a limited number of goods and services.

Using round numbers and data provided by the US government, Gross Domestic Product rose by less than 13% from 2007 through 2012 while the money supply, M2, rose by 36%.* The USA is creating dollars much faster than it is creating economic goods and services. This sets the stage for significant inflation in the future.

* Data taken in June 2012 from:

http://www.federalreserve.gov/releases/h6/20120503/

http://www.whitehouse.gov/sites/default/files/omb/budget/fy2013/assets/hist.pdf p.212.

H6 statistical release for June 14 2012 from the Board of Governors of the Federal Reserve System
http://www.federalreserve.gov/

Appendix C - Paths to Prosperity

Political hardball is real, and it is rare to see a politician miss a chance to score political points. However, some situations are so significant that it would be valuable to pull back from the political battles enough to see shared goals. Improving prosperity is one of those shared goals. Fill a room full of liberals, conservatives, Libertarians, etc. Ask the people if they would like to see a more prosperous America. You should get total agreement.

Make the matter a little more precise. Define prosperity as lower unemployment and a higher rate of growth of GDP. You will still get massive agreement.

Having established a shared goal of a more prosperous America, we can now look at the competing paths to prosperity offered by the Democrats and the Republicans. The paths are exceptionally different, and we should consider them with care as we make our choices about the future. Here is a brief presentation of the two different approaches:

The Republican Approach

Principles:

> Prosperity is achieved through the entrepreneurialism and the energy of self-interested actors in a free market.

> Increasing prosperity, (lower prices plus more goods coupled with low unemployment), requires the expansion of supply.

> Government enhances prosperity by providing security, a means to settle disputes, and basic infrastructure.

> Governments are emphatically ill-equipped to craft economic plans that achieve prosperity through government programs, mandates, or centralized planning

Assessment of the Present Situation:

> Government spending levels are too high.

> The growing debt burden is unsustainable.

> Regulatory complexity and tax code complexity diminish supply.

> Businesses are uneasy in part because our government chastises and demonizes successful businesses.

GOP proposals:

> Reduce Federal spending levels to 2006 levels.

> Simplify taxes (Fair tax or Flat tax)

> Reduce regulatory burdens (Take President Obama at his word. http://www.whitehouse.gov/the-press-office/2011/01/18/improving-regulation-and-regulatory-review-executive-order.)

> Reinforce the idea that the federal government should be limited.

The Democratic Approach

Principles:

> Prosperity requires a partnership of business and government.

> Increasing prosperity requires the expansion of demand.

> Government spending is a significant component of prosperity.

> Government should invest in future technologies.

> Government needs to balance efforts to increase prosperity with vital social concerns.

Assessment of the present situation:

> Government spending levels are about right.

> Government revenues are too low.

> Businesses are not investing as they should.

> The tax code is insufficiently progressive.
The rich need to be taxed more.

Democratic Proposals:

> Maintain spending at and gradually above 2012
levels.

> Increase taxes on tax payers earning more than
$250,000.

> Use government subsidies and direct investments
to promote R&D into favored areas.

> Use government subsidies and direct investments
to invest in certain technology and infrastructure.

> Simplify certain regulations, but maintain the
benefits of government oversight.

> Reinforce the idea that government expertise is a
required part of coping with a complex economy.

Some facts to help evaluate the paths

As one engages in a debate about the effectiveness of the two approaches, one often sees the need to refer to some economic facts. Here is some data taken from various government web sites that should help.

(All data are from US govt. sources)

US Deficits		Fed Revenue	Fed Outlays
2005	318 Billion	2,154 Billion	2,472 Billion
2006	248 Billion	2,407	2,655
2007	161 Billion	2,568	2,729
2008	459 Billion	2,524	2,983
2009	1,413 Billion	2,105	3,518
2010	1,293 Billion	2,163	3,456
2011	1,300 Billion	2,303	3,603
2012	1,327 Billion	2,467 est.	3,796 est

GDP in Billions of 2005 Dollars

2004	11,676
2005	12,429
2006	13,207
2007	13,861
2008	14,334
2009	13,938
2010	14,360
2011	14.959
2012	15,600 (est.)

Unemployment rate in June 2012 - 8.2%

Share of individual income tax paid by the top 20% of all households in 2005 was 86.3%

Share of individual income tax paid by the top 20% of all households in 2007 was 86.0%

In 2005, you were in the top 20% if your adjusted gross income was $88,030 or more.

.....

Share of individual income tax paid by the top 5% of all households in 2005 was 60.7%

Share of individual income tax paid by the top 5% of all households in 2007 was 61.0%

In 2005, you were in the top 5% if your adjusted gross income was $157,176 or more.

Who Paid Their Fair Share of Taxes?

ESTIMATED FEDERAL INCOME TAXES PAID IN 2009, BY INCOME GROUP

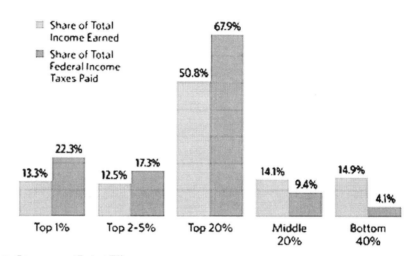

Source: Congressional Budget Office

http://blog.heritage.org/2012/07/12/cbo-report-confirms-rich-already-pay-their-fair-share/
Guinevere Nell, July 12 2012

,,,,,,,,,,,,,,,,,,,,,,,,,,,,

Caution: As we consider the economic facts and circumstances concerning segments of the population, such as "The top 5% of income earners", we can easily fall into the trap of thinking we are talking about the same people over time. That is not the case. The individuals making up any economic segment will change over time.

For instance, a person who is graduated from college in June and who takes a starting position in a company in October will have a very modest amount of taxable income to report for the year. That person will almost certainly be among the bottom 5% of income earners for the year. However, the situation should change for that person over time, even though there will always be a "bottom 5%".

The same reasoning can apply at the upper end. A widow who sells the family farm or business could very well be in the upper 1% of income earners for that year but fall out of that category the very next year.

,,,,,,,,,,,,,,,,,,,,,,,,,,,,,,

In the February 2012 edition of Reason magazine, Veronique de Rugy cited tracking of the 675,000 people reporting income in excess of $1 million in 1999. Half of them had dropped out of that category by 2000. Only 15% remained in the second year, 2001, and 8% were left by the third year, 2002.

One can use the principles and the facts presented above to make an informed judgment about which path is more likely to succeed.

I argue the facts show we have a spending problem.

I add support to the argument that we are overspending by noting the following assertions:

A. No country has been able to use government spending to create long term prosperity. In fact, just the opposite happens. (See Weimar Germany, Argentina, or, recently, Greece and Portugal. The history of the UK also offers rich examples.)

B. In the short term, government deficits create the illusion of growth because the spending adds to the GDP. However, this is the same as what happens when a family thinks it is doing better because it can use credit card borrowing to support a life style beyond its means. The future is bleak in both cases.

C. The argument that government can invest in our future depends on the hope that government decision makers are wise enough to make good investment choices. When you consider that the actual people making those choices are people who are good at being elected or people who are good at being appointed by elected officials, you have to acknowledge our government decision makers do not have any particular talent or skill to cause them to make wise economic investment decisions. Look at Freddie Mac and Fannie Mae for examples.

D. When private programs or investments do not pan out, investors take steps to stop the bleeding and look for better options. When government programs or investments do not pan out, we typically argue that more money needs to be invested. Look at public education as a long term example. Look at the recent stimulus package for a short term example.

Appendix D - Tax on Repatriated Profits

American companies with operations in other countries face an unusual tax situation dealing with profits earned in the foreign country.

Let's consider this situation by imagining an American company with a subsidiary in a European country. The corporate tax rate in the European country is 20 percent. The corporate tax rate in the USA is 35 percent.

If an American company earned $100 million in profits from its operations in Europe, it would pay corporate income taxes to the host European country. The American company would pay $20 million in taxes and retain $80 million in after tax profits.

The American company can leave the $80 million in Europe, if it wishes, and that ends the tax impact. The $80 million can be invested in expanded operations anywhere except in the USA. The company can hire additional employees and make additional capital investments abroad as it wishes.

However, if the American company were to send the $80 million back to its US headquarters, for whatever reason, it would have to pay an additional income tax. American law would require the American company to pay an extra $15 million to the US government, causing its corporate tax rate on the $100 million in before tax profits to rise to the

102

American rate of 35%. The American company would be left with $65 million in after tax profits in the USA.

Thus, the American company can have $80 million in after tax profits if it keeps its earned profits abroad, or it can have $65 million if it wants to bring the profits back to the USA.

Not surprisingly, many American companies choose to keep the money abroad. Even if the company doesn't have a need to invest in its foreign operations, it is wiser to keep the $80 million in foreign bank and investment accounts rather than to lose $15 million (18.75 % of $80 million) the instant the money is transferred to the USA.

The tax on repatriated profits earned abroad is a fence that keeps hundreds of billions of dollars from being brought back to the USA where they might be spent in the American economy. Revenues from the repatriation tax must be low as a wise finance officer would never recommend repatriating substantial profits.

The elimination of the tax on repatriated profits would be a welcome move for those who want to promote the American economy. Literally hundreds of billions of dollars would be permitted to be returned to the USA without an additional tax penalty. It should be clear that the American economy would benefit from having that money at home, for whatever purposes, rather than having that money stay abroad.

Proponents of keeping the repatriation tax in place offer two arguments.

The first argument is that the existence of the tax pressures companies to remain in the USA rather than to create subsidiaries in other countries. That is a thin argument. having to keep one's profits abroad is a small penalty to pay for enjoying a 20% tax on profits rather than a 35% tax.

The second argument is that there is no guarantee American companies would use all or most of the repatriated profits to invest in new jobs. That is true, but puzzling. Forcing the money to remain outside the USA means that all investment, jobs or spending derived from that money will take place in other countries. Certainly, that situation is not helpful to the USA and its economy or its job seekers. Wouldn't it be to the benefit of Americans, including American job seekers, to have the profits earned outside of the USA returned to the USA?

A prosperous economy, with stronger employment, requires robust and profitable business operations in the USA. If one seeks prosperity in the USA, one should not complain that repatriation of profits earned abroad would enhance businesses in the USA, nor should one try to tie the repatriation to certain conditions. Money is fungible. Money brought to the USA, for whatever purpose, enhances the American economy.

Appendix E - Fiscal Reform - Budget Issues

Fiscal choices (how much the government should spend and how much the government should tax) are exceptionally prominent at the time of the writing of this essay. The USA's national debt in the summer of 2012 (roughly $16 trillion) exceeds the Gross Domestic Product, and US deficits are adding about $1.4 trillion to that debt each year at our present rate. (Estimates vary, but the Federal government will spend over $3.7 trillion in 2012 with revenue near $2.3 trillion.) Both Democrats and Republicans use the term "unsustainable" to describe this situation. The American government cannot continue to spend massively more than it collects in revenues.

What is to be done? In order to answer that question, one must first understand some of the basic components of spending and taxing in the USA.

Spending

The federal government's budget can be divided into two broad categories, discretionary spending and non-discretionary spending.

Discretionary Spending: Discretionary spending is spending that is appropriated and authorized each year in the budget law. For instance, the federal office of the National Endowment for the Arts requested a budget of $146 million for 2012. All, some or none of that requested amount can be included in the budget law for 2012 when it is enacted.

Non-discretionary spending: The federal government has passed laws to define certain conditions that trigger government spending. For instance, the Medicare program is required to pay certain health care costs for all pregnant women and all children under the age of six if their family income is lower than 133% of the poverty level. (There are other conditions that trigger Medicare coverage as well. This is just an example.) The law doesn't say, "We will pay X dollars for Medicaid." It says we will pay when certain conditions apply. That means the payment is mandatory, and the amount is uncertain. Medicaid, Medicare, Social Security, certain unemployment benefits, and interest on borrowed money are examples of non-discretionary spending. Information from the President's Office of Management and Budget shows at least 61% of the 2012 budget proposal is in the area of non-discretionary spending.

The non-discretionary part of the budget is growing rapidly. The federal debt is growing, which means the mandatory interest payments are also growing. The number of citizens over 65 is increasing, which means expenditures for Social Security and Medicare are rising. Expenditures required by the Patient Protection and Affordable Care law, ("Obamacare"), remain to be understood and weighted.

The expanding amount of mandatory spending, coupled with the need to include a certain amount of discretionary spending (for agencies such as the State Department, the

Treasury, and the Department of Defense, among others) creates a growing price tag for all federal spending. At present rates of spending and of revenue to the federal government, the deficits remain large, hence the concern that the situation is unsustainable. Continuing deficits and a growing national debt will wreck the American economy.

Going back to the question "What is to be done?", one sees that the federal government must find ways to balance its budget. A budget in deficit can be brought back into balance by spending less, collecting more revenues, or a combination of the two.

Dealing with Deficits by Spending Less

Cutting government spending is something most people can favor as a general principle. (Note: There are some who disagree and who argue that additional government spending, even deficit spending, is a useful tool to promote economic growth.) However, deciding what spending is to be cut generates substantial difficulty and major political resistance. Every spending item has supporters who enjoy the financial benefit of spending that is steered their way. Politicians who propose to cut a favored program will lose political support from the special interests that benefit from the program and gain only tepid political support from the rest of the voters.

Social Security, Medicare and Medicaid are large government programs that have strong support from the beneficiaries, and the beneficiaries have a track record of assigning their political support only to politicians who promise not to diminish those programs. The beneficiaries also like politicians who expand those programs, so our lawmakers have substantially augmented these programs over the decades. The beneficiaries' political support for their programs is so large that such programs, particularly Social Security, have been called the "third rail of politics." (Subway trains and other electric-powered trains ride on two rails and use a third rail to carry the electric current. Touching the third rail will kill you.)

The value of the benefits promised in Social Security and Medicare vastly exceed projected revenues. While the situation is too complex to permit precise calculations, the sizes of the "unfunded obligations" are clearly staggering. Denis Cauchon of USA Today reported the gap between Social Security benefits and taxes to be $21.4 trillion based on today's population. He also reports unfunded Medicare costs will amount to $24.8 trillion over 20 years. (http://www.usatoday.com/news/washington/2011-06-06-us-debt-chart-medicare-social-security_n.htm 7 June 2011 Article by Denis Cauchon.) Unfunded Medicaid and other health care costs must be in similar situations.

Americans have avoided dealing with the problem of excess spending and promising. The phrase "kicking the can down the road" is used to describe how the American government has responded to the looming projections of future fiscal difficulty by finding ways to get by for another year or until the next election. Given the size of the fiscal deficits and the mass of the national debt, it is becoming harder and harder to "kick the can down the road."

Although it is becoming harder to avoid having to deal with the fiscal situation, the political difficulty of cutting spending or promises remains powerful.

As one considers what might be done concerning Social Security, Medicare and Medicaid, it is important to recognize we do not have the option of keeping everything as it is. These three entitlement programs are built on promises that simply cost more than we can sustain in the future.

What about the discretionary part of the budget? Can substantial spending be cut there? Well, one can certainly argue there is room for cuts. (Why is our government proposing to spend approximately $5 billion on an alternate engine for the F-35 fighter, an idea not supported by the Department of Defense? What is the constitutional basis for the existence of the National Endowment for the Arts? Etc.) However, finding "room for cuts" and actually cutting are two different things.

As with non-discretionary spending, discretionary spending programs earn strong political support from various beneficiaries and interest groups. Politicians who propose or support cuts in discretionary spending programs face substantial organized opposition.

The conclusion is that our political system historically favors increases in spending and does not favor cuts in spending. The results of the 2010 election suggest we might be experiencing a change. Perhaps we have reached a point where the typical American voter is ready to offer support to budget cutters. Perhaps not. The future will tell.

I must note one final bit of data. Cutting spending enough to eliminate the $1.4 trillion budget deficit would still leave the government $2.3 trillion to spend. That would put spending levels near where they were in 2005. While it would be difficult to live within our means, one cannot look at government service levels as they were in 2005 and argue that they were horribly inadequate. It would be politically difficult to make the spending cuts needed to eliminate the deficit, but one should not think such cuts would be "draconian."

Dealing with Deficits by Increasing Revenues

Having seen the magnitude of the spending side of the problem, and having recognized the challenge of reducing spending, we can now turn to the revenue side of the issue. What could be done to cope with the deficit problem by generating larger government revenues?

One simple observation is to note that government tax revenues will increase if prosperity expands in the USA. Strong economic growth would generate additional income streams and jobs. Tax revenues would increase, and, as an additional benefit, spending for unemployment and low-income programs would decline.   (Appendix C, "Paths to Prosperity", presents the divergent ideas about how to encourage economic growth.)

110

Conservatives offer a "supply side" approach to expanding the economy. They expect reduced regulations and reduced taxes will encourage businesses to make products, sell services and hire people.

Liberals offer a different approach. They expect increased government spending to stimulate economic growth, and they expect government investments in selected technologies will result in general expansion of the economy.

Another quick observation is that perhaps one ought to be able to increase government revenues by increasing tax rates and by adding additional taxes. This is the path offered by many Democrats and liberals. Let's consider the idea of increasing tax rates and adding new taxes.

Taxing More - The Problem of Unintended Consequences and Real Numbers

What would happen if the government tried to bring the budget into balance by increasing taxes and tax rates? Given that the deficit is estimated to be $1.4 trillion, balancing the budget through taxation would require taxes to bring in $1.4 trillion above the current revenue levels of $2.3 trillion. $1.4 trillion is an astonishing number. It is nearly 10% of the entire GDP. It is two thirds of all current government revenues. If the government were to impose additional taxes or higher tax rates designed to generate additional revenues to close even a third of the deficit, the impact on the economy would be major.

One reason large tax increases would have a major impact on the economy is that money extracted by taxes must come from somewhere else. If government tax laws are altered and cause the government to collect extra revenues, for the sake of argument let's say an extra $500 billion, then that $500 billion had to be diverted from some other purpose or activity. $500 billion more in tax revenues implies $500 billion less in consumer spending or savings and investment. While some might argue the government could employ that $500 billion more wisely than the private sector, decades of experience with collectivism and central planning around the world shows otherwise. Economic health and growth would diminish as a result of steps taken to increase government tax revenues.

Another reason large tax increases would have a major impact is that people alter their behavior when faced with significant economic factors. One highly noticeable step people make in the face of higher taxes is to move. (The Internal Revenue Code even has a section, section 877, that deals with tax-motivated expatriation.) Many businesses also select or move their headquarters or their operational locations in part because of tax codes (and other regulations). Additionally, when facing large taxes, people study the laws in order to adjust their actions to minimize the tax bites. The altered behavior not only reduces the projected tax revenues, but the changed behavior often also means people deviated from economic choices they would have made had taxes not been a major factor. In other words, tax considerations could lead people to make choices that are less than optimal except for the tax considerations. Obviously, the economy is not well served when people make less than optimal choices.

Increasing taxes on the rich:

Now let's consider proposals to increase taxes on the rich. Populist politicians have long enjoyed political advantage by targeting "the rich." The massive deficit we face in the USA has renewed calls to close the gap by extracting more from the rich.

In his message about the 2012 budget proposal, President Obama wrote:

I continue to oppose the permanent extension of the 2001 and 2003 tax cuts for families making more than $250,000 a year and a more generous estate tax benefiting only the very largest estates. While I had to accept these measures for 2 more years as a part of a compromise that prevented a large tax increase on middle-class families and secured crucial job-creating support for our economy, these policies were unfair and unaffordable when enacted and remain so today. I will push for their expiration in 2012. Moreover, for too long we have tolerated a tax system that's a complex, inefficient, and loophole-riddled mess. For instance, year after year we go deeper into deficit and debt to pay to prevent the Alternative Minimum Tax (AMT) from hurting many middle-class families. As a start, my Budget proposes a 3-year fix to the AMT that is paid for by an across-the-board 30 percent reduction in itemized deductions for high-income taxpayers. My Administration *will work with the Congress on a long-term offset for these costs.*

(http://www.whitehouse.gov/omb/overview retrieved 20 June 2011

The Obama administration proposes to increase the tax rates of the highest two tax brackets by eliminating the "Bush tax cuts" for the rich. The highest tax rate would increase from 35% to a new rate of 39.6%. (This rate includes those earning over $379,000.) The second highest rate would increase to 36% from its present level of 33%.   (This tax rate includes individuals earning over $175,000 but under $379,000. The bracket is from $212,000 to $379,000 for the category of "married, filing jointly.") In addition, the Obama administration proposes to eliminate certain tax deductions from those whose income exceeds certain levels.

Using 2008 data, the latest data published by the IRS (at the time this was written), the proposed tax rate increases would collect an additional $34 billion if nothing else changes. (Remember, however, that people certainly will change their behavior in the face of increased tax rates. This number represents, therefore, the maximum additional tax revenue that would be raised by the increased tax rates.)

I cannot put a figure on the potential revenue changes that would result from the elimination of certain tax deductions, but it seems President Obama's proposals to raise tax revenues by extracting more revenue from the rich might generate somewhere around $100 billion or so. That is well short of the amount needed to cut the $1.4 trillion deficit by increasing revenues.

What would be required to use the rich to make up the $1.4 trillion deficit? We can answer that by looking at the IRS data. We will consider "the rich" to be households and small businesses with reported taxable income of $200,000 or more.

In 2008, (the last year for which the IRS posted data at the time this was written), 4,359,936 households and small businesses submitted tax returns showing adjusted gross income of $200,000 or more. The total adjusted gross income on these returns was $2,058 billion. The total tax was $531 billion.

(data taken from http://www.irs.gov/taxstats/indtaxstats/article/0,,id=133521,00.html 23 June 2011)

Put another way, after paying $581 billion in taxes, those reporting incomes of $200,000 or more where left with a total reported income of just over $1.5 trillion. In other words, virtually all of their reported income would be required to close the $1.4 trillion deficit. There are simply not enough of "the rich" available for us to tax our way into a balanced budget.

One must conclude that trying to close the $1.4 trillion deficit through increases in tax revenue will require the government to take more in taxes from many people who are not considered to be "rich."

(As this essay indicates, trying to close a $1.4 trillion deficit largely through taxes is impractical, and it would have adverse impacts on the economy as a whole. That is not to say that our present tax structure is fine as it stands. It is not. The complexity of the present tax code is such that Americans have to devote perhaps as much as $200 billion a year just to handle tax reporting and preparation. The structure of the tax code opens the door to concerns that it lacks fundamental fairness. The business taxes are the highest (or second highest, depending on how you calculate them) in the world, creating an uncompetitive situation. Accordingly, tax reform measures to simplify the code, broaden the base of taxpayers, and lower the tax rates would be welcome. Such measures could have an impact on expanding the economy and the corresponding tax revenues, but that is different from trying to increase tax revenues by adding taxes or increasing tax rates.)

Combination of spending cuts and revenue increases:

Given the size of the deficit, it is tempting to think the solution will require a combination of spending cuts and revenue increases. From a liberal perspective. this makes sense. Liberals believe the government can employ money more appropriately than money is employed by businesses or "the rich." Therefore, taxing away some of that money would be a wise way to close some of the deficit gap. Given the Left's preference for static

116

economic analysis, increasing tax rates and adding taxes would raise government revenues and diminish pressures to cut government spending.

From a conservative perspective, dealing with the deficit through a combination of spending cuts and revenue increases makes sense provided one expects the revenue increases to come from economic growth. (The economy will suffer if the government merely increases tax rates or adds new taxes. The economy will grow and revenues will increase if the government broadens the tax base, reduces tax rates and reduces the regulatory burden.)

Conclusion

The political debate about how to deal with the deficit is, and will continue to be, heated. It is clouded by the fact that the debate is not just about an economic matter, it is also about political power for the Left or the Right.

The point of this essay is to clarify some of the key points of the debate and to note that both sides of the political debate agree the underlying economic situation is unsustainable. The economic foundations of the USA will suffer the longer the government continues to engage in deficit spending.

Appendix F. Laffer curve and tax rate revenue effect.

The Laffer curve is a concept developed by the economist Arthur Laffer. It explains the relationship between income tax rates and government revenues from income taxes.

The concept starts with a simple graph showing tax revenues on the vertical axis and tax rates on the horizontal axis. We will use that graph to show the relationship between tax rates and government revenues. Quite obviously, a tax rate of zero will generate zero revenue (Point A on the graph). A tax rate of 1% will generate a small amount of revenue (Point B), and a rate of 5% will generate more revenue (Point C).

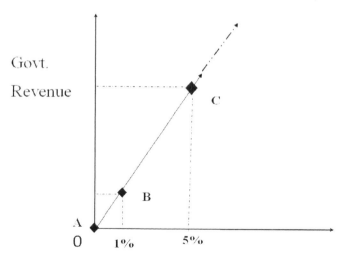

It is tempting to think that revenue will continue to climb as tax rates are increased. However, let's give that idea some careful thought. What will happen at a tax rate of 100%? Will the government enjoy years of high revenues? No. As soon at a 100% tax is enacted, people will stop working, and the government's revenues will fall to zero (Point D). At a rate of 90%, some people would continue to work. There would be some revenue to the government, but not much (Point E).

We see that the curve representing the function of government revenue at particular tax rates starts climbing as taxes rise beyond zero, but it is falling as taxes approach 100%. Obviously, there has to be a point (the inflection point) where the curve switches from a rising one to a falling one. We can draw a notional graph of the function as shown below:

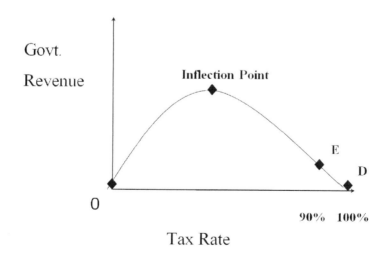

Please recognize this sketch shows a concept. We lack the data to define the shape of the curve with precision.

Now let's consider what happens if our tax rates are already beyond the inflection point. Look at Point F on the graph. It represents the revenue (R1) generated at a 70% tax rate. What happens if the government increases the tax rate to 75% (Point G)? Revenue falls to R2! This represents the key message of the Laffer Curve.

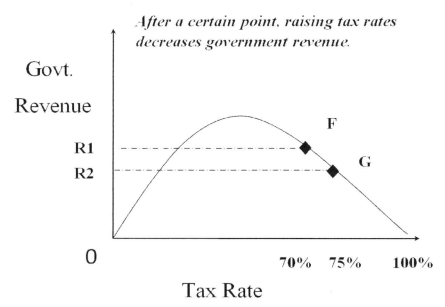

If you want to increase government revenues, and you are already charging high tax rates, you should decrease the tax rates.

Why does this work? it works because our economy is dynamic, not static. People react to things. Behavior changes. Higher taxes reduce the rewards earned through hard work and extra work. Why put out the extra effort if much of the benefit will be taken away? In addition, our tax codes are complex and contain legal methods to reduce taxes. At high tax rates, people hire CPAs to help them learn how to alter their behavior and reduce the tax bite.

Additional information can be found from an article written by Arthur Laffer in June 2004. It can be found at:

http://www.heritage.org/research/reports/2004/06/the-laffer-curve-past-present-and-future

Appendix G
Budget Proposals for 2012 & 2013

(Shown on next pages)
President Obama's 2012 proposal
President Obama's 2013 proposal
House Budget Committee proposal 2012 (Republican)
House Budget Committee proposal 2013 (Republican)

Table S-1. Budget Totals

(In billions of dollars and as a percent of GDP)

	2010	2011	2012	2013	2014	2015	2016	2017	2018	2019	2020	2021	Totals 2012-2016	Totals 2012-2021
Budget Totals in Billions of Dollars:														
Receipts	2,163	2,174	2,627	3,003	3,333	3,583	3,819	4,042	4,257	4,473	4,686	4,923	16,366	38,747
Outlays	3,456	3,819	3,729	3,771	3,977	4,190	4,468	4,604	4,876	5,154	5,422	5,697	20,134	45,952
Deficit	1,293	1,645	1,101	768	645	607	649	627	619	681	735	774	3,269	7,205
Gross domestic product (GDP)	14,508	15,060	15,813	16,752	17,782	18,804	19,791	20,755	21,679	22,624	23,608	24,633		
Budget Totals as a Percent of GDP:														
Receipts	14.9%	14.4%	16.6%	17.9%	18.7%	19.1%	19.3%	19.5%	19.6%	19.8%	19.9%	20.0%	18.3%	19.0%
Outlays	23.8%	25.3%	23.6%	22.5%	22.4%	22.3%	22.6%	22.5%	22.5%	22.8%	23.0%	23.1%	22.7%	22.7%
Deficit	8.9%	10.9%	7.0%	4.6%	3.6%	3.2%	3.3%	3.0%	2.9%	3.0%	3.1%	3.1%	4.3%	3.7%

This is a page of President Obama's 2012 budget request as presented by the Office of Management and Budget.

http://www.whitehouse.gov/omb/budget/Overview

The 2011 figures are estimates.

The 2012 figures are requested, but the 2012 budget law has not yet been passed.

The figures for 2013 and beyond are projections by the OMB.

123

Table S–1. Budget Totals

(In billions of dollars and as a percent of GDP)

	2011	2012	2013	2014	2015	2016	2017	2018	2019	2020	2021	2022	Totals 2013–2017	Totals 2013–2022
Budget Totals in Billions of Dollars:														
Receipts	2,303	2,469	2,902	3,215	3,450	3,680	3,919	4,153	4,379	4,604	4,857	5,115	17,167	40,274
Outlays	3,603	3,796	3,803	3,883	4,060	4,329	4,532	4,728	5,004	5,282	5,537	5,820	20,687	46,959
Deficit	1,300	1,327	901	668	610	649	612	575	626	678	681	704	3,440	6,684
Debt held by the public	10,128	11,578	12,637	13,445	14,198	14,990	15,713	16,404	17,137	17,897	18,678	19,486		
Debt net of financial assets	9,170	10,467	11,368	12,023	12,653	13,281	13,894	14,469	15,066	15,753	16,433	17,137		
Gross domestic product (GDP)	14,959	15,602	16,335	17,196	18,178	19,261	20,369	21,444	22,421	23,469	24,427	25,488		
Budget Totals as a Percent of GDP:														
Receipts	15.4%	15.8%	17.8%	18.7%	19.0%	19.1%	19.2%	19.4%	19.5%	19.7%	19.9%	20.1%	18.9%	19.2%
Outlays	24.1%	24.3%	23.3%	22.6%	22.3%	22.5%	22.2%	22.0%	22.3%	22.5%	22.7%	22.8%	22.6%	22.5%
Deficit	8.7%	8.5%	5.5%	3.9%	3.4%	3.4%	3.0%	2.7%	2.8%	2.9%	2.8%	2.8%	3.8%	3.3%
Debt held by the public	67.7%	74.2%	77.4%	78.2%	78.1%	77.8%	77.1%	76.5%	76.4%	76.3%	76.5%	76.5%		
Debt net of financial assets	61.3%	67.1%	69.5%	69.9%	69.6%	69.0%	68.2%	67.5%	67.2%	67.3%	67.3%	67.2%		

124

S-1 FY2012 BUDGET RESOLUTION
(NOMINAL DOLLARS IN BILLIONS)

	2011	2012	2013	2014	2015	2016	2017	2018	2019	2020	2021	2012-2021
Outlays	3,618	3,529	3,558	3,583	3,667	3,855	3,996	4,123	4,354	4,547	4,745	39,958
Revenues	2,230	2,533	2,860	3,094	3,237	3,377	3,589	3,745	3,939	4,142	4,354	34,870
Deficit	-1,388	-995	-698	-489	-431	-478	-407	-378	-415	-405	-391	-5,038
Debt Held by the Public	10,351	11,418	12,216	12,797	13,319	13,876	14,351	14,787	15,242	15,673	16,068	n.a.

As a Share of GDP

	2011	2012	2013	2014	2015	2016	2017	2018	2019	2020	2021	10-Year Average
Outlays	24.1	22.5	21.7	20.8	20.2	20.1	19.9	19.7	19.9	19.9	19.9	20.5
Revenues	14.8	16.1	17.4	17.9	17.8	17.6	17.9	17.9	18.0	18.2	18.3	17.7
Deficit	9.2	6.3	4.3	2.8	2.4	2.5	2.0	1.8	1.9	1.8	1.6	2.7
Debt Held by the Public	68.8	72.8	74.5	74.2	73.2	72.5	71.6	70.6	69.7	68.7	67.5	71.5

11 April 2011 summary of House budget proposal
http://budget.house.gov/uploadedfiles/summarytables.pdf

125

FY2013 Path to Prosperity
(NOMINAL DOLLARS IN BILLIONS)

House Budget

	2012	2013	2014	2015	2016	2017	2018	2019	2020	2021	2022
Outlays	3,624	3,530	3,476	3,536	3,690	3,824	3,977	4,199	4,409	4,605	4,888
Revenue	2,444	2,734	2,980	3,232	3,449	3,642	3,811	3,986	4,184	4,388	4,601
Deficit	1,180	797	496	304	241	182	166	213	225	217	287
Debt Held by Public	11,355	12,261	12,861	13,260	13,597	13,874	14,126	14,417	14,717	15,005	15,364

As a Share of GDP

	2012	2013	2014	2015	2016	2017	2018	2019	2020	2021	2022
Outlays	23.4%	22.2%	21.0%	20.1%	19.7%	19.4%	19.3%	19.4%	19.5%	19.5%	19.8%
Revenue	15.8%	17.2%	18.0%	18.3%	18.4%	18.5%	18.4%	18.4%	18.5%	18.6%	18.7%
Deficit	7.6%	5.0%	3.0%	1.7%	1.3%	0.9%	0.8%	1.0%	1.0%	0.9%	1.2%
Debt Held by Public	73.2%	77.0%	77.6%	75.3%	72.7%	70.4%	68.4%	66.7%	65.1%	63.5%	62.3%

Summary of House budget proposal (Ryan Plan)

July 2012 http://budget.house.gov/fy2013prosperity/

Appendix H - The Budget In Perspective

The budget of the Federal government is so big the numbers hardly make sense. A billion dollars is such a huge number, we cannot really comprehend it, and a trillion dollars is so much worse. A good way others have used to get a grip on the budget is to cut off the last eight zeroes to reduce the scale of the Federal budget to the scale of a household budget.

Here is the Federal Budget for 2012 from President Obabma's 2013 budget proposal:

Revenue - $2,469 Billion
Spending - $3,796 Billion
Deficit   - $1,327 Billion

In July 2012, the total national debt is $15,887 Billion

Chopping off eight zeroes generates the following picture of the Federal budget at the scale of a household budget:

Income $24,690
Spending $37,960
Borrowing $13,270 (additional credit card debt)

Credit card debt owed: $158,870

Looking at the budget from this perspective helps us to understand just how out of balance and serious the present situation is.

Appendix I - Jo Ray's Economic Solutions

Economics and Politics can often appear to be daunting and complex. Every time I feel overwhelmed by the complexity, I can rely on the common-sense wisdom of my wife. She has looked at our economic crisis and decided a few simple steps will put us on the path to recovery.

Here they are:

1. No more borrowing. We can't spend ourselves out of debt. It is immoral to pass a huge debt to our children and grandchildren. Live within our means. Families do it, and the politicians can too. By the way, just living within our means isn't good enough. We had better start paying down the debt.

2. Let's grab the low-hanging fruit. Get rid of the tax on repatriated profits. All that money is being used in other countries. That's silly. Let it come home. It can be spent, invested or whatever. I want it to be working here, not in some other country.

3. Repeal Sarbanes-Oxley. That law drives business out of the USA and prevents foreign businesses from coming here. It costs billions of dollars in compliance, and it doesn't seem to be doing any real good. After all, the crooks at Enron were prosecuted perfectly well under the pre-SOX laws.

4. Democrat Alice Rivlin, the first head of the Office of Management and Budget, had some fine ideas we should adopt. First, go to a two year budget instead of a one year budget. Have you seen the nonsensical spending that happens at the end of every fiscal year as agencies rush to spend all their money so they can ask for more? How absurd! A two year budget cycle would reduce that absurd behavior by half. Next, require Congress first to vote on the total amount to be spent. Then they will have to pick priorities. The present system of "additions to the baseline" and "adding all the requests" makes little sense

5. Cut business taxes to zero. We consumers pay those taxes anyway, so stop kidding yourselves into thinking the businesses are the ones who pay. What do you think foreign businesses would do if the business taxes in the USA went to zero? Why, there would be a stampede of foreign businesses rushing to establish themselves right here. In addition, home-grown business creation would grow. Job growth would soar. The economy would surge. Revenues from other taxes would make up for the loss of revenue from business taxes.

6. Reform the tax code. What we have is grotesque. No one knows what is in the mass of law and regulations we call our tax system. We spend tons of money (over $200 billion a year) just trying to comply with tax rules, and, at the end of the day, we all wonder if we have reported correctly, and we're pretty sure some people are getting over by finding sneaky exceptions and provisions in the complex code. Throw it all out. Replace it with the Fair Tax or with a simple Flat Tax.

7. Repeal many regulations. We have masses of regulations, and we keep making more. The regulatory mess was created with good intentions, but it has gotten out of hand. Now it is stifling economic activity and lots of other actions as well. The President should require the Cabinet secretaries to review the regulations managed in their departments in order to simplify and reduce them. A 20% cut in the first year should be the goal with more to follow. (President Obama has ordered a regulatory review, but it seems to have stalled. If his order was anything more than political fluff, he should be calling his Cabinet members to ask them what part of his order they did not understand.)

8. Pass a Balanced Budget Amendment. Our Congresses and our Presidents have not been good stewards of our economy. They have spent and spent and spent. They have shown they cannot use their power properly, and they have shown their personal political needs outweigh a wholesome respect for the future economic health of the nation.

9. Stop demonizing the successful. Does our administration really want people to become successful? Let's see, if you manage to earn more than $200,000 you are not paying your fair share, and you probably lack a proper dose of common decency and concern for your neighbors. The administration wants to fix that. If you are a major industry or corporation, "Big Oil, Big Pharma, Big Banks, Big Auto, Big Insurance, Big anything", you merit scorn and potential government control or take-over. That atmosphere does not encourage innovation, investment,

entrepreneurialism or an energetic pursuit of economic success. That can't be good for the health of our economy.

10. Pass a term limits amendment for both houses of Congress. Too many Representatives and Senators seem to be focused on re-election. Holding the seat means power and a good life. Too many of them use Federal spending to help them keep their seats. That is not what the Founders had in mind. Members of Congress should not be able to make a career out of getting re-elected and staying in Washington. We can debate the details of the limits, but the goal should be to have people briefly serve in Congress as a duty, not a life style.

Jo Ray has more ideas, but this is a good start. I am impressed by her ideas about political reform as well, but that is the topic for another essay.

Appendix J -- A Technical Concern About the Recovery

The USA is currently experiencing a most unsatisfactory "recovery". It is a "jobless recovery" and a recovery that is not generating any economic energy to speak of.

Perhaps it is not a recovery at all. Perhaps dramatic new levels of "monetizing the debt" by the Federal Reserve Board are skewing our normal method of measuring economic growth. Let me explain.

Economists define a recession as a period of two or more quarters of declining economic activity. A recovery is the period of increasing economic activity following a recession. Changes in economic activity are measured by changes in Gross Domestic Product, GDP.

The Gross Domestic Product is a measure of the value of all sold products and services produced in the USA. It's about $15 trillion.

Economists measure GDP by taking the sum of C (spending on Consumption of goods and services by households and businesses) plus I (spending on Investment) plus G (Government spending) plus Ex (spending on goods and services made in the USA but exported) minus Imports.

Focus for a moment on G, government spending. In the past, funds used for government spending were acquired through taxes (which diverts money out of the

132

Consumption stream) or through borrowing from financial markets (which diverts money out of the Investment stream.) GDP remained generally unaffected in the short term because increases in G (government spending) were offset by decreases in C (consumption) or I (investment). One could argue the government was merely using its taxing and borrowing powers to shift consumption and investment choices to public goods and services rather than the goods and services citizens and businesses would choose individually. The measurement of the strength of the economic engine, GDP, would not be altered.

However, in the past three years, our government has behaved quite differently. In addition to normal borrowing from financial markets, the government now borrows massively from itself by selling notes to the Fed. The Fed buys US Treasury notes, but it uses "money" that it simply creates by adding numbers to its own accounts. (This is called "monetizing the debt" or "printing money".) This practice allows an increase in government spending, but there is no corresponding diversion from investment spending.

If the Fed creates $900 billion this way, (as it has), and the government spends it, G grows artificially, and measured GDP will also grow. (Artificially creating $900 Billion and adding it to government spending represents a growth of 6% of a $15 Trillion economy.) That growth is deceptive. It does not represent an expanding economy any more than a family could pretend its annual income rose by $1,000 because it was able to spend $1,000 drawn from a credit card. (The analogy is stretched because the Fed is not using a credit card. It is just creating the money.)

Governments would love to be able to expand their economies simply by creating and spending more money, but that path never has worked, and it cannot work now.

The USA is presently in a technical recovery. Reported economic growth is about 2% per year for the past three years. Intriguingly, 2% per year for three years matches the 6% artificial growth measurement caused by monetizing the debt.

The recession is reported to be over, but the recovery seems weak and thin. People ask, "where are the jobs?" What is going on? Well, part of the problem may be the artificial growth of GDP caused by the Fed's monetizing the debt. If the underlying engine of our economy really were growing, even at just 2%, we would be seeing better job growth and something like a real, if modest, rebound. However, if the economic "growth" is largely an artificial numbers game, ... ah... that's a different matter.

We know monetizing the debt will result in future inflation. Perhaps an additional, "unintended", consequence of monetizing the debt is the creation of the illusion of a growing economy by skewing the measurement of GDP. If so, that would help to explain why so many Americans don't see much joy in this "recovery".

134

Appendix K - Cost of Wars

Defense Spending since 1900

Defense spending in the United States has fluctuated in the last century, rising from one percent of GDP, peaking at 42 percent in World War II, and declining from 10 percent in the Cold War to five percent today.

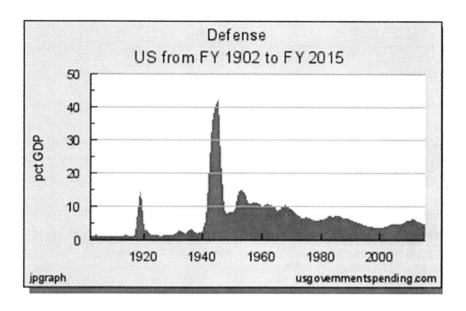

Federal Defense Spending 1902-2015

The defense establishment that sent the White Fleet around the world before World War I was tiny, compared to the defense establishment of mid century. It was about 1.25 percent of GDP. Yet this tiny establishment was expanded into an expeditionary army in World War I that consumed over 14 percent of GDP and turned the tide of the war in France. After the war the armed forces were rapidly demobilized, and defense spending returned to about 1.25 percent of GDP.

Then in World War II the United States achieved an unprecedented mobilization of resources, and defense spending rose to 42 percent of GDP in 1945. But after the war it never returned to previous levels. From a low of 7.33 percent of GDP in 1948 it doubled to 15 percent at the height of the Korean War in 1953 and was maintained at about 10 percent during the peak of the Cold War through the end of the Vietnam War. Against this, the defense buildup during the Reagan era, from 5.6 percent of GDP in 1979 to 7 percent of GDP in 1986 was modest, and the Bush buildup from 3.6 percent in 1999 to 6 percent in 2010 to fight the first battles against Islamist extremism equally restrained.

The plans of the Obama administration show a reduction in spending back to 4.6 percent of GDP by 2015.

The information above came from http://www.usgovernmentspending.com/past_spending 1Nov 2011. It is printed here with permission.

Estimated War-Related Costs, Iraq and Afghanistan

According to the Center for Defense Information, the estimated cost of the wars in Iraq and Afghanistan (starting from 2001) will reach **$1.29 trillion** by the end of fiscal year 2011.

(See the next page for a chart.)

Source: "The Cost of Iraq, Afghanistan, and Other Global War on Terror Operations Since 9/11," Amy Belasco, Congressional Research Service Report for Congress, RL33110).

http://www.infoplease.com/ipa/A0933935.html 1 Nov 2011

(Cost of wars in billions of budgeted dollars)

Operation	FY 2001+ 2002	FY 2003¹	FY 2004²	FY 2005³	FY 2006	FY 2007	FY 2008	FY 2009	FY 2010	FY 2011	Total
Iraq		$53.0	$75.9	$85.5	$101.6	$131.2	$142.1	$95.5	$65.9	$51.1	$802
Afghanistan	20.8	14.7	14.5	20.0	19.0	39.2	43.5	59.5	104.9	119.4	455.4
Enhanced security	13.0	8.0	3.7	2.1	0.8	0.5	.1	.1	.1	.1	28.6
Unable to allocate		5.5									5.5
Totals	$33.8	$81.2	$94.1	$107.6	$121.4	$170.9	$185.7	$155.1	$171.0	$170.7	$1,291.5

Source: "The Cost of Iraq, Afghanistan, and Other Global War on Terror Operators Since 9/11," Amy Belasco, Congressional Research Service Report for Congress, RL33110)

http://www.infoplease.com/ipa/A0933935.html 1 Nov 2011

Appendix L - The Bill of Rights

(Or should it be called the "Bill of Limitations"?)

The first ten amendments to the Constitution

Amendment I

Congress shall make no law respecting an establishment of religion, or prohibiting the free exercise thereof; or abridging the freedom of speech, or of the press; or the right of the people peaceably to assemble, and to petition the Government for a redress of grievances.

Amendment II

A well regulated Militia, being necessary to the security of a free State, the right of the people to keep and bear Arms, shall not be infringed.

Amendment III

No Soldier shall, in time of peace be quartered in any house, without the consent of the Owner, nor in time of war, but in a manner to be prescribed by law.

Amendment IV

The right of the people to be secure in their persons, houses, papers, and effects, against unreasonable searches and seizures, shall not be violated, and no Warrants shall issue, but upon probable cause, supported by Oath or affirmation, and particularly describing the place to be searched, and the persons or things to be seized.

Amendment V

No person shall be held to answer for a capital, or otherwise infamous crime, unless on a presentment or indictment of a Grand Jury, except in cases arising in the land or naval forces, or in the Militia, when in actual service in time of War or public danger; nor shall any person be subject for the same offense to be twice put in jeopardy of life or limb; nor shall be compelled in any criminal case to be a witness against himself, nor be deprived of life, liberty, or property, without due process of law; nor shall private property be taken for public use, without just compensation.

Amendment VI

In all criminal prosecutions, the accused shall enjoy the right to a speedy and public trial, by an impartial jury of the State and district wherein the crime shall have been committed, which district shall have been previously ascertained by law, and to be informed of the nature and cause of the accusation; to be confronted with the witnesses against him; to have compulsory process for obtaining witnesses in his favor, and to have the Assistance of Counsel for his defense.

Amendment VII

In Suits at common law, where the value in controversy shall exceed twenty dollars, the right of trial by jury shall be preserved, and no fact tried by a jury, shall be otherwise re-examined in any Court of the United States, than according to the rules of the common law.

Amendment VIII
Excessive bail shall not be required, nor excessive fines imposed, nor cruel and unusual punishments inflicted.

Amendment IX
The enumeration in the Constitution, of certain rights, shall not be construed to deny or disparage others retained by the people.

Amendment X
The powers not delegated to the United States by the Constitution, nor prohibited by it to the States, are reserved to the States respectively, or to the people.

Appendix M
Pressures to Expand the Power of Government

The threat to the continued existence of the USA as a republic and to Americans' rights as individuals comes, in large part, from the pressures to augment the power of government or to weaken the restrictions on government established by the Constitution.

Here are five factors or pressures leading to the augmentation of government power:

A. The lure of Statism: It is very tempting to believe that government is composed of wise people who can handle the difficult challenges of the day. American Liberals are happy to embrace that idea, and Republicans frequently join them. It does not matter that our government officials and administrators really do not possess extraordinary capacities, nor does it matter that so many government programs suffer from inefficiency and ineffectiveness. The lure remains strong.

B. Lure of the Nanny State: It is also very tempting to believe the government should take care of our needs, (be the nanny state). Politicians promise easy results, if only the voters will elect them. Once elected, those politicians too often find Constitutional limitations to be excessively restrictive. They work around the limitations and stretch the "elastic clauses" so much that the limitations become meaningless. (See Appendix N for a discussion of the "elastic clauses".)

C. While the lures of Statism and of the Nanny State are strong, the appreciation of the value of rights and Liberty is weak. Who speaks of Liberty any more? Who fears the oppressive power of government?

George Washington is supposed to have said:

"Government is not reason, it is not eloquence, it is force. Like fire, it is a dangerous servant and a fearful master…"

We never hear such notions today. No, many of our citizens see only the "helping hand" of government. Our ancestors prized Liberty and earned it for us. We, however, lacking any experience or understanding of just how oppressive government can be, do not cherish Liberty for its own sake.

D. A fourth factor is the demise of respect for the individual and the rise of emphasis on groups. (See "Identity Politics".) (See the Federalist Papers and concern about "factions.)

D. A fifth factor is the growing intrusion of government into economic matters. As the government controls ever larger portions of the economy, so will it also control ever larger portions of daily life. A combination of socialist views, egalitarianism and "crony capitalism" (not to be confused with normal Capitalism) can wreck the free market and erect a dominant state in its place.

Appendix N - Elastic Clauses

There is substantial debate about the appropriate reading or interpreting of the Constitution. Some see the Constitution as a "living document" that can be shaped to meet modern needs without having to go through the difficult amendment process. Some, the "Strict Constructionists", argue we must treat the Constitution as law and read just what is written, not what we imagine. Others, those who argue for "Original Intent", say the words of the Constitution should be interpreted through the lens of the intentions the Founders had in mind.

Whichever of these views you favor, if you are interested in the role of the Constitution as a fundamental document guiding and limiting the power of the Federal government, you will soon encounter the "elastic clauses" contained within the Constitution.

The "elastic clauses" have been used by the Congress and the courts to "stretch" the powers of the Federal government. This appendix argues that the three "elastic clauses" are not really as "stretchy" as some would argue.

The **"Commerce Clause"** is a powerful elastic clause. The Constitution grants to the Federal government the power to "regulate interstate commerce". That power was granted to avoid the situation that could arise when one state tries to tax goods from another state through tariffs. It has been stretched to justify everything from banning guns in school to banning the growing of wheat for personal consumption. (See www.lawnix.com/cases/wickard-filburn.html for the Wickard v. Filburn case about wheat.) In the recent debate about the Affordable Care Act, some argued the Commerce Clause granted the Federal government the power to force citizens to buy something.

If, as some would say, the Commerce Clause grants the Federal government authority to exercise its powers any time there is an exchange of goods and services, or any time there ought to be an exchange of goods or services, then there really is no limit at all to what the government can do. The Founders need not have bothered enumerating the powers of government if the Commerce Clause was intended to grant the Federal government power to act so pervasively.

A second elastic clause is the **"necessary and proper"** clause. The Constitution grants the Federal government power to do what is necessary and proper to perform obligations of the Federal government specified in the Constitution.

Article One, Section 8 says, in part, "Congress shall have the power.... To make all Laws which shall be necessary and proper for carrying into Execution the foregoing Powers, and all other Powers vested by this Constitution in the Government of the United States, or in any

145

Department or Officer thereof."   The clause itself is sensible. For example, Article I of the Constitution grants to Congress the power to coin money. One can imagine a number of related laws would be required to shape how the Congress was to go about arranging for the coining of money. The "necessary and proper" clause, operating within a framework of respect for the limitations established elsewhere by the Constitution, is not troublesome. When the fundamental limitations and boundaries have been breached, however, then the "necessary and proper" clause can be used to justify a substantial expansion of Federal power .

The third clause I call to your attention is the **"General Welfare"** clause found in the preamble and in Article 1 Section 8.

From the preamble: : "WE THE PEOPLE of the United States, in Order to form a more perfect Union, establish Justice, insure domestic Tranquility, provide for the **common defense**, promote the **general Welfare**, and secure the Blessings of Liberty to ourselves and our Posterity, do ordain and establish this Constitution for the United States of America."

From Article 1, Section 8 : "The Congress shall have the Power to lay and collect Taxes, Duties, Imposts and

146

Excises, to pay the Debts and provide for the **common defense and general welfare** of the United States, but all Duties, Imposts and Excises shall be uniform throughout the United States. . ."

I have highlighted the words "Common Defense" and "General Welfare" to make a point. If you go among the English speaking people of the world, you will rarely hear the phrase "common defense" except from Americans. The adjective "common" is not needed for a single country. Why was it used in our Constitution? It was used to make the point that the Federal government had to provide for the defense of **all** of the states, not just one, two or a few. (This reflects the natural worry of the delegates to the Constitutional Convention that their states not be "short changed" by the exercise of Federal power. The Federal power was to be used to the benefit of all states, not just some.) By the same token, the "General Welfare" does not mean "welfare in general". It is a term that is best understood as the opposite of "Specific Welfare". Laws are to be crafted to serve all states, not just specific states. (The end of the quotation from the Constitution reinforces this idea by emphasizing that taxes are to be uniformly applied. You see the determination to ensure Federal powers are not captured to serve the interests of only a single state or a group of states.)

Our misunderstanding of the General Welfare clause causes us to think it says, "welfare in general" rather than the "common or shared welfare". That error allows the Federal government to claim the power to act in areas well beyond those enumerated in the Constitution.

Appendix O - Personal Finance

I offer this section to provide information to individuals as they cope with personal financial decisions.

Basic Personal Finance

"A wealthy man spends a dollar less than he earns. A poor man spends a dollar more than he earns."

Everyone has to cope with financial decisions. Such decisions can range from dealing with very basic considerations to investing in highly complex arrangements. The purpose of this paper is to help people understand basic financial matters. The complex issues will not be touched.

Basic Financial Goals

Imagine starting out on your own. What are your financial goals? The proper basic goals are simple. First, you have to live within your means. Second, you have to prepare for unexpected problems. Third, you have to prepare for the long range future. (You can move beyond these basic goals and build plans to start a business or to reach goals associated with wealth, but that is a different topic.)

Living within your means

Many people get into financial difficulty because they spend money without a plan. They buy what they need and what they want. Then something unexpected comes along, and they spend more. Before you know it, they are in debt and in trouble. You can avoid this by planning what to do with your money. A budget is the key tool to help you make that plan.

Budgeting is a simple concept. You start with your income. Then you decide what your minimum savings must be. (You do plan to save, don't you? The future is uncertain. You need savings to deal with the unexpected.) Finally, you allocate the rest to cover your expenses. Almost certainly, you will want to spend more than you have. You will have to establish priorities. Your needs come first, then you can start spending on wants. The budget process helps you establish your priorities.

Expenses - When first building a budget, people often fail to think of all of the expenses they face. Here are some common categories for you to consider: Taxes, Savings, Debt Payments (student loans, credit cards), Food, Utilities (electricity, water, natural gas, sewage, trash) , Car (gas, insurance, payments, repairs, tax), Lodging, Phone, Internet, Household Supplies (cleaning, small repairs, paper products), Medical Expenses (insurance, co-payments, over-the-counter, dental, self-insured events), Special Savings for Defined Future Purchases (car, house, TV), Charity, Church, Personal Care Products, Clothing, Gifts, etc.

Notice the expense list is pretty long, and it hasn't yet included entertainment, eating out, hobbies and other fun stuff.

The list also changes when you have children. Once you start to raise a family, the list of expenses will grow. That is why it is a good idea to eliminate debt and build savings before starting a family.

Of course, after you create a budget, you have to track your expenses to see if you are sticking with the budget plan you made. The information you get from tracking your real expenses will lead you to make some adjustments to the budget. It should also help you develop discipline to follow your budget.

Hmmm... that "simple budget concept" just became tricky, didn't it? At this point, many people give up. Building a budget is too hard for them, and tracking expenses is just too bothersome. Almost all of these people will wind up spending more than they earn, borrowing to cover their excess spending, and digging a deep financial pit. Once they finally wake up, they will have to endure a period of serious austerity as they try to recover by taking extra jobs and drastically cutting back on expenses.

Credit Cards - Credit cards deserve special attention. A credit card is a lousy tool for borrowing. The interest rates charged for carrying a credit card balance are high. On the other hand, a credit card is a fine substitute for carrying cash. If you pay the monthly balance in full each month, you pay no interest at all. My wife and I have done that for over forty years... except for the month I put the payment envelope in my pocket and failed to mail it. (blush) If you are carrying a credit card balance, pay it off as quickly as you can and never create another one.

Preparing for Unexpected Problems

You created a budget to allow you to live within your means, and you are tracking your expenses to help you follow your plan. However, life is full of uncertainties. I do not know what odd expenses will land in your lap, but I am confident something will happen. It could be an illness, an unanticipated repair, the loss of your job, or anything else. You need to have an emergency fund saved up to help you cope with the problem.

How big should the emergency fund be? There is no certain amount. Suggestions vary between three and six months of after tax income. Obviously, you cannot put that much away instantly, so you have to build it up over time. I recommend that you tighten your belt in the first years in order to build at least three months worth of savings as soon as you can.

Where should you put that money? Emergency fund money needs to be invested, but you also need to be able to use it quickly. (We say an investment is "liquid" if you can get at the money quickly.) Savings accounts in a bank or credit union are highly liquid. Of course, they do not carry a high interest rate right now, so they are less than ideal. I recommend using a savings account to start your fund and then shift it to a "money market account" once you have built up $1000 in savings. (See the investment section below to learn about money markets.)

Early Death - An early death is an unexpected event. If you have no obligations to others, you can set this concern aside. However, if you have a family, and people are depending on your income, then an early death becomes an "unexpected problem" that merits attention. The best way to deal with that problem is through term life insurance. (See the Insurance section below.)

Preparing for the Long Term Future

Someday you expect to retire. You must prepare for that. Social Security is NOT a proper retirement plan. The structure of Social Security is, as they say, "unsustainable". That means the present form of Social Security cannot exist in your retirement future. Your retirement funds must come from your savings and investments while you are working.

In addition to retirement, you may have some other long term goals which require savings and investment.

So, how should you save and invest to meet these needs?

The first thing to consider is any retirement plan offered by your employer. Some employers offer matching funds for employees who contribute money to a retirement plan. (These plans are typically called 401K or 403B plans.) If that is the case, and you do not make the required contribution, you are throwing away the matching money. Therefore, the obvious thing to do is to make at least the minimum contribution needed to generate the matching contribution from the employer.
Once you have made sufficient contributions to generate any matching contributions, you should consider adding

more. Alternatively, you can put any additional funds into other investments. At this point, it is necessary to discuss investment options.

Investment Options

When we save money, we are merely putting it aside so we can spend it later. If we were to take some cash and put it under the mattress for several years, we could spend it in the future. However, the cash we put away would steadily lose buying power due to inflation. Inflation happens because the amount of money created in a time period is greater than the amount of money needed to purchase the additional goods and services created in the same time period. This results in more dollars chasing each thing we want to buy which causes prices to increase. (The average price of a gallon of milk in Maine in Jan 2006 was $2.88. In Jan 2011 it was $3.59. http://www.maine.gov/agriculture/mmc/prihis.htm) Because of inflation, the purchasing power of a dollar in the future is less than the purchasing power of a dollar today.

Because of inflation, we want any money we save or set aside to earn interest at a rate that will at least match the rate of inflation.

Simply saving money in a mattress or a bank is not our only option. We might also let that money be used by someone else, just as we might let someone else use a summer house we are not living in. People "rent" other peoples' money by paying an interest rate for the use of the money. All sorts of investment options exist that allow savers to put their money to work at interest rates that will, hopefully, be better than the rate of inflation. Of course, these investment options also carry risks.

In general, investments with higher rates of interest also carry higher risks. Investors have to balance their hope to enjoy certain interest payments against the risk that all or part of the money they invested (the principal) will be lost.

There are many vehicles to use to invest saved money. This section will provide you a quick look at the basic saving and investment vehicles. These are just the basics. Each vehicle can be offered with a variety of additional features.

You should not be intimidated by your lack of knowledge about any investment vehicle. Ask questions about anything you do not understand. Do not put your money into anything you do not understand. If someone tries to pressure you into making an investment, run away!

Interest Bearing Checking Accounts: A checking account is just a way for you to let a bank hold some of your money and then deliver it to whomever you authorize. When you write a check, (paper or electronic), you authorize the bank to send the money to the designated payee. Sometimes banks will offer a small interest payment to encourage customers to use their checking accounts. The interest rates on these accounts are quite small. They are an inducement to use one bank instead of another, but they are not large enough for us to think of interest bearing checking accounts as investments or even as good ways to save. These accounts are normally insured up to $250,000 against the failure of the bank, so the investor can be confident the money will not evaporate. (Check to see if the account is "FDIC Insured".)

Bank or Credit Union Savings Accounts: Savings accounts are straight forward. You put money in the account, and the bank pays you a certain amount of interest. You can withdraw the saved money when you want. Typically, savings accounts carry modest interest rates that are generally near the rate of inflation. (Caution. For the past several years, interest rates have been remarkably low.) You can hope the dollars you save will hold most of their purchasing power, but you should not expect much, if any, growth. Normally, these accounts are also FDIC insured.

Other Bank Accounts: Some banks and credit unions offer accounts that mix the effect of savings and checking. They may also limit the number of checks per month or require minimum balances or other things. These accounts will have various interest rates or withdrawal penalties associated with them. Think of them as checking or savings accounts with extra features. In general, the bank will offer you a slightly higher interest rate if you keep a certain balance and if you let the bank use the money for a longer time. You can decide if the interest rate advantage is worth the limitations on your flexibility.

Certificates of Deposit: Banks offer CDs. For example, a bank might offer you 1% interest if you promise to invest $1,000 for a year or 1.3% if you invest $5.000 for three years. The interest rate offered will generally be higher than the savings rate. Longer periods of investment command higher interest rates than shorter periods. There are penalties if you have to get the money before the period expires. CDs can be FDIC insured.

As you should be noticing, the banking instruments above are, at best, means to save. They do not offer the extra interest needed to allow purchasing power to grow. (Of course, the risks are almost zero as well.) The investment vehicles below carry greater hope for gain and greater risks as well.

Money Market Accounts: Business and banks often need to use large amounts of money. A money market account is a vehicle that lets small investors pool their money to be used by larger business or banks. If you open an investment account with a stock broker, you will probably have the option to allow your unused cash to be swept into a money market account. Money market accounts generally have better interest rates than bank savings accounts, and they carry some risk as well. The interest rates are, typically, still quite low. (I use a money market account as a useful place to keep money that I am not yet ready to invest in other investment vehicles. My brokerage firm automatically puts dividend and interest payments as well as proceeds from stock sales into my money market account rather than have the cash build up in my brokerage account.)

Stocks: Stocks are part ownership shares of a company. A company issues a certain number of shares of stock. Those shares are bought and sold in stock exchanges. Shares are most commonly traded in blocks of 100 shares. (Smaller amounts can also be bought or sold if one is willing to pay a higher fee or commission on the trade.) You can buy or sell shares of stock through companies called brokerages. Some brokerage companies offer advice. Some do not. Some charge higher commissions than others.

A person who buys shares of stock in a company hopes to gain in one or both of two ways.

The first way is through dividends. If the company earns profits, the shareholders may vote to distribute all or some of the profits to the shareholders. Each shareholder would receive a certain amount of money called a dividend.

The second way is through appreciation. If the value of the stock goes up in the stock market, the shareholder could sell his shares at the new price, pay the sales commission, and hope to have made more than he paid for the stock. (This is called a capital gain.)

Buying stocks carries risks. There is no real guarantee of any dividends, and the value of the stock can fall. Some people invest in stocks because they have confidence in the underlying purpose and functioning of the company. Some people "play the market". They look at market indicators and try to time their buying and selling. The actual company doesn't matter much if the technical indicators look right. (I call these people "gamblers".)

Mutual Funds: Most investment advisors suggest that investors spread their investments among several investment vehicles. That way if one investment vehicle falters (remember the risk?) an investor will not lose everything. Of course, it can be hard for a single investor to spread his small investment among several investments. A mutual fund is way to pool investors' money and use it to invest in a defined set of investment vehicles. (For example, a mutual fund might be set up to buy only small companies with potential for growth.)

If 100,000 people invest $100 a month into an investment fund, the fund managers would have $10 million to invest every month. The managers could spread that investment amount among many investment choices. Each investor would own a small part of the total fund, but that small part would be spread among many investments.

 As with stocks, investors buy a part of the mutual fund. Investors can get sell their share of the mutual fund at any time by selling their fund shares.

Funds come in many varieties. For the moment, just look at two major categories, "load" and "no-load". A "no-load" fund can be bought and sold without paying an extra commission. Stick with those for now. Mutual funds also charge fees, and the fees vary, so check that as you shop.

Remember that investing in stocks or in mutual funds carries risk. You could lose everything you invest. What you just read is a major simplification. There are many varieties of mutual funds and many varieties of rules. You are welcome to learn more, and you probably will. If you are investing in a retirement plan, you are probably going to be asked to choose several places to put your retirement money. These are almost always mutual funds.

Bonds: Governments and companies often need to borrow money. They do so by selling bonds. For instance, Ford Motors might sell a bond that is its promise to pay the holder (bearer) of the bond $10,000 on May 30th, 2020. An investor would want to pay less than $10,000 for that bond. Investors bid on the bond when it is first issued. Investors who own bonds do not have to wait for the bonds to expire. They can sell them in the secondary market. In general, if interest rates go up, the value of the bonds will decline. If interest rates go down, the value of the bonds will increase.

The risk associated with bonds is attached to the viability of the company or government that issued the bond. Bond rating agencies try to assess that risk by issuing ratings, such as AAA or AA, to indicate the rating agencies' confidence that the company or government will repay the bond.

Prior to the US government take-over of General Motors, bonds were a stronger investment than they are now. If a company got into trouble, bond holders had a higher claim on assets than did shareholders, management or unions. The US government changed that by placing the union claim above the claim of bond holders when it "bailed out" GM.

IRAs, Roth IRAs, 401K and 403B Retirement Accounts: Individual Retirement Accounts and 401K or 403B retirement accounts are special cases. They allow people to gain tax advantages while investing for retirement.

For example, if I have $300 a month taken out of my pay and invested in my 403B, my taxable income for the year is reduced by $300 a month. (My 403B investment uses pre-tax dollars.) In addition, interest earned by my 403B account is not taxed in the year it was earned. I only have to pay taxes when I retire and start to withdraw money from the account. (One expects to be in a lower tax at retirement.)

In return for those tax advantages, an investor would have to pay large penalties if the money is withdrawn before retirement age. There are some differences among the retirement account options, so read up on them when you confront the choice of how to invest for retirement. Funds in these retirement accounts typically are invested in mutual funds.

Real estate: Some people invest in real estate. They buy property to rent to others. They hope the value of the property will appreciate over time. This method of investing has been around for a long time. It got a very bad name recently because the "housing bubble" drove

161

property values higher than they should have been. Many people lost money during the correction that happened when that bubble burst. ("Bubbles" are a part of life. We had the "dot-com" bubble and the housing bubble in recent times. There will be others. I just don't know what they will be.)

Some people like to pool their money and buy real estate through something like a mutual fund. These funds are called Real Estate Investment Trusts, (REITs), and they invest in property instead of stocks. Shares in REITs can be purchased through brokerages and retirement funds.

Other Investment Vehicles: There are lots of other ways to invest. One can invest in options, gold or commodities, for example. These investments go beyond the scope of this paper. Look into them after you have digested the basics.

Life Insurance
Notice I did not include life insurance in the investment section.

Life Insurance comes in two general forms, term insurance and "whole life" insurance.

Term insurance is simple. I bought a $500,000 term life insurance policy when I was much younger. The policy is set to expire (its "term" ends) when my wife and I are 65. If I die before then, she gets the $500,000 and can use that to sustain her and our children until our retirement plans are mature. If I live to the end of the term, then the policy evaporates. My monthly premiums are what I pay for the assurance that my family would be sustained if I die.

 Whole life is a bit different. Whole life insurance policies are more expensive than term insurance policies. However, a whole life policy doesn't evaporate at the end of the term. Instead, the holder of a whole life policy who lives to a certain age will enjoy a stream of income or a lump sum payment.   Because of this, whole life insurance is sometimes marketed as an "investment".   I rejected whole life insurance policies because I could make much more money by investing the difference in premiums myself. Insurance agents warned me that many people lack the discipline to invest the difference, so the whole life plans could be wise because the investment is automatic.

In my case, term life insurance was the right choice. I have invested the difference in the premium values, and my investments have earned a substantially greater return than the feeble rates of return offered by whole life insurance.

When should you buy life insurance? If you are single, you do not need any at all. if you are married to a person who works or can work, you do not really need life insurance until you have children. Once you have children, you probably need life insurance to care for them until they are old enough to lead their own lives.

Scams
If it seems too good to be true, then it probably isn't.

Sadly, the investment world includes horrible investment options and scams. I could never catalog the sorts of scams you might encounter. However, I can offer some indicators that should help you recognize a scam. An appeal to greed is the first indicator. There is no such thing as an investment option with low risk and guaranteed high rates of return. (... and if such an opportunity actually existed, why would this fine person whom you never met before be offering it to you instead of making the investment himself?) Time pressure is the second indicator. If someone is warning you to invest quickly before the golden opportunity expires, you should probably back out of the deal. The third indicator is upfront money. If the deal requires you to pay special fees or provide lump sums right away, it might be a bad deal. (Some proper investments actually do require front-loading of the investment, so this indicator is not absolute.) The final indicator is secrecy. If you are asked to keep quiet about the deal, or if you are told that the deal is only for a special set of investors, you are almost certainly being set up.

Advisors

There are a variety of people and organizations that offer investment advice. Some advice is free. Some advice carries a price tag. Obviously, some advice is good, and some is not. I ask you to remember there are no guarantees, and advisors cannot relieve you of the responsibility for your decisions and actions.

Listen to advice. Ask questions when you do not understand. (It is easy to become embarrassed and to accept what you are told rather than reveal your ignorance or uncertainty. Please fight that tendency.) It is your money, and you need to be comfortable that you understand whatever situation you are considering.

If an advisor pressures you, be cautious.

If an advisor wants to control your investment, be cautious.

If an advisor makes exciting promises, be cautious.

It is wise to know how an advisor earns his money.

Conclusion

Investments offer rewards and carry risks. You have to balance those. If you cannot afford to lose some money you have gathered, then put it in a bank or a CD or a money market account. When you have gathered some money that you can afford to invest, check your options. Ask questions. Diversify your investments. Let time work for you by investing early and withdrawing late.

John Van Vliet